Education can be big business. Companies compete to put out the best learning management systems online, market textbooks that are tied to state standards, and trumpet their prowess in increasing engagement or decreasing absenteeism. What is too often missing from this business, however, is heart and passion and purpose. Steve Perkins' book of musings, reflections, and wisdom restores the humanity to our classroom practice and provides a necessary counterweight to the attitude that students are clients and parents are customers. Perkins sees education as Plutarch did, not as the filling of a bottle but as the kindling of a fire. His essays, like his stellar career in the classroom, are characterized by humility and generosity. You won't come away from the book with a ready-made lesson plan, but you will take away something even greater by reading it—joy.

Ed Coleman
Milken Educator and National Board Certified Teacher
Maggie L. Walker Governor's School, Richmond, Virginia

Through the lyrical and intelligent tone that is classic Steve Perkins, this book paints his personal and practical experiences from the classroom with an introspective, almost reverent hand. Here, a reader will find real people doing the real and remarkable work that good educators do daily. The takeaways are all rooted in truth, that if such goodness is happening in the classrooms we visit in this book, then such must be true elsewhere too, which means there is a reason for hope. An unforgettable read!

Kathy Nimmer
2015 Indiana Teacher of the Year
Director of SEEDS
Tippecanoe School Corporation, Lafayette, Indiana

In *The Golden Waffle Principle: Finding Meaning in Teaching*, Steve Perkins draws from classroom experiences, classical literature, and "salt of the earth" wisdom to masterfully weave together didactic tales that are sure to inspire and encourage. Those who know Steve are sure to imagine his booming, gregarious, yet humble voice narrating these nuggets of gold. *The Golden Waffle Principle* will draw you in as you discover the profound impact that being a teacher with a love of teaching, learning, students, and of course all things Latin can have. Perkins ultimately blurs the lines between storyteller and philosopher, redefining educational excellence in the process. This book is an ode to education.

David McGinness, EdD
Director of Student Teaching
Assistant Professor of Education
Taylor University, Upland, Indiana

As a teacher and leader in Australian schools for nearly 40 years, making "connections in all directions" has framed my instinctive drive to lead with trust, conviction, love, laughter and high expectations. I commend this book to anyone in life who loves to make "connections in all directions". Author Steve Perkins will lift you out of your seat as you levitate in this land of descriptive passages and transform you to a world of deliciously written essays and experiences where you will experience grandeur on a grand scale. Education is indeed grand – from the curious look from a child, a poignant question from a teenager, an electric spark from a teacher, or a contented sigh from a leader contributes to what manifests our profession to be magical and grand. These essays will broaden your mindset because of the eloquently chosen words, the passage of rich experiences and the connections between intellect and love. A must have for all home bookshelves and libraries around our world.

Kate Smith
Principal Palmerston District Primary School, Canberra, Australia
2000 National Excellence in Teaching Awards – for Inspirational Teaching
2013 National Excellence in Teaching Awards – for Inspirational Leadership
2014 - Harvard Club of Australia Recipient for Leadership Excellence

Artfully connecting the modern classroom to ancient wisdom, *The Golden Waffle Principle* celebrates the timeless pursuit of knowledge while exploring the premise that education is far more than the mere dissemination of it. Get ready to rediscover the true magic of teaching. Through thoughtful reflections and expert insights, this award-winning teacher will bring you into the depth and beauty of what it means to teach like never before. Drawing on an illustrious career spanning decades of classroom and higher education teaching experience, Perkins offers profound ways to look at the essence of teaching, learning, and school.

Gary Abud, Jr.
2014 Michigan Teacher of the Year
Author of *Science With Scarlett*
Detroit, Michigan

The Golden Waffle Principle: Finding Meaning in Teaching

Published by Cogrounded, Inc.
325 E. Grand River Avenue
Suite 300
East Lansing, MI 48823
cogrounded.org

ISBN: 979-8-9919316-1-8

Produced in the United States of America

Cover Design and Book Layout by Austin Perkins
Typeset in Baskerville Regular, Sharp Sans Extra Bold

For more information from the author, please visit: stevenrperkins.com

For information about special discounts for bulk purchases, please contact: grow@cogrounded.org

Library of Congress Cataloging-in-Publication Data

Perkins, Steven
The Golden Waffle Principle / Steven R. Perkins
5.5" x 1" x 8.5"

Education, Philosophy

First Edition
2024

The Golden Waffle Principle:
Finding Meaning in Teaching

Steven R. Perkins
Indiana Teacher of the Year

To all who hear and follow the call to "Train up a child in the way he should go: and when he is old, he will not depart from it."
(Proverbs 22:6, KJV)

Contents

Philosophy and Education

Introduction

In the first essay of this book, you will find the core philosophy of the Golden Waffle principle, namely that words can serve as a kind of linguistic time-binder – something that can capture the essence of an image, idea, or experience from one place and time and communicate it in another. Words are not unique in this, for a taste or smell can evoke vivid images within us or call to mind certain memories as well, but words, both written and spoken, are the most common and most powerful vehicles for transporting ideas.

When I was a boy, I used to spend time with one of my grandmothers, and we would swing on her front porch as she told stories or we sang songs together. One of the songs we enjoyed was the African-American spiritual "Swing Low, Sweet Chariot." As the swing carried us back and forth and we sang, "I looked over Jordan, and what did I see," I assumed that Jordan was the name of the next street over from the one on which my grandma lived, for that is what we were looking toward as we sang the line. The words of that song bound an idea and planted it firmly in my mind, and that idea remained for many years until I learned that "Jordan" meant something else entirely and that the street one block away from my grandma's house was called Vest Street. Yet now, despite knowing all about the Jordan River and the roads of my grandma's neighborhood, whenever I hear that great hymn, I am instantly transported to that porch swing. In my mind's eye, I see that street one block over, where I still halfway expect "a band of angels comin' after me."

Welcome to The Golden Waffle Principle, a powerful metaphor to remind us that words are powerful transmitters of ideas. It is also a metaphor to spark a question: What do you think of when you hear the word "teaching?" Or "school?" Or "education?"

Article 9, Section 1 of the original constitution for the state of Indiana describes education as a "grand object." Why is that? Why did those founders of a midwestern state view education so highly? Why have most people around the world and throughout time held a similar view? Is that a phrase you would use when you think about education today?

This is not your typical education book, at least it is not typical these days. It does not contain references to the latest theories and research. It lacks any kind of charts, tables, or note-containing data. In fact, most of the authors it cites have been dead for several hundred years, even a millennium or more.

As for organization, it does not have sections devoted to themes, although I had considered that at one point. This book is more like the poems of Catullus, the epistles of Seneca, or the essays of Montaigne in that its contents flow from one idea to another, sometimes returning to an earlier notion or going off in an unexpected direction. In that regard, it is like life, certainly the life of the classroom.

Most of these essays are taken from my blog, *Magister's Musings*, intoy2014.blogspot.com, which I launched when I was named the 2014 Indiana Teacher of the Year (INTOY). The first period of the school day had started, and the first-year Latin students were just into their opening activity when I noticed a crowd of people at my door. Suddenly my room was invaded by our principal and superintendent, news crews from Indianapolis television stations pushed into the room, and the Indiana Superintendent of Public Instruction announced to my students that their teacher was the new

Indiana Teacher of the Year. I made a beeline for my wife and children, and the picture on the front page of the *Indianapolis Star* shows me hugging them tightly. In truth, I was squeezing them for dear life. As the circus that was enveloping me endeavored to whisk me away for a press conference, my first thought was about the students sitting in the room, so I asked if a class cover had been arranged. Everyone laughed, and my superintendent assured me there would be a substitute teacher for the entire day.

At that first press conference there were many smiles and pictures and questions, but there was one question that nearly threw me. Someone asked what I planned to do with my upcoming sabbatical. No one had told me about this, and I no longer remember how I replied, but the 2006 Indiana Teacher of the Year, my friend and colleague Louisa LaGrotto, later explained that I would have the option of taking the year off to work at the Indiana Department of Education. It was an option I would eventually decline.

My place was in the classroom, and while I did arrange to be away numerous days the following year visiting schools around Indiana, I was not interested in working on World Language curricula for the IDOE. In fact, when the dust had settled on the day of my INTOY announcement, I dismissed the substitute teacher and returned to my room to teach my afternoon classes. I will never forget Nick, one of my seniors in Advanced Placement Latin, telling me at the end of class how much he appreciated that I had come back to teach that day.

Perhaps that is a deeper reason why I have chosen to portray a centurion in my work as a historical reenactor. My character is that of Gaius Crastinus, a centurion in Julius Caesar's tenth legion. We know little about him, which leaves me freedom to discuss many things about Roman army life in my portrayal, but it is important to note that a centurion was the highest-ranking enlisted man in the ancient Roman army. Higher offices were often reserved for senators or members of the Roman elites, but a centurion worked his way up from the ranks of the raw recruits and continued to serve on the front lines with his men. This is how I see my role in the world of education. I have been blessed that my recognitions have opened many doors for me to work with extraordinary people across the United States and beyond, and I do feel a responsibility to lead more broadly, but my primary work will always be on the front lines, which is to say, among the desks of my students.

As for that broader leadership, I have had the opportunity to mentor many student teachers and others in the profession. For a time, I co-hosted an education podcast with my good friend and 2014 Michigan Teacher of the Year, Gary Abud, Jr. I have also maintained my blog, *Magister's Musings*, and that is where this book comes in. I am humbled that more than 130,000 people have read it and that many have taken the time to leave comments. I pulled together the most popular posts and from those have chosen the ones that speak most clearly to how I have come to see education in a career of more than three decades. I have made some changes to those original posts, updating references and expanding ideas in a way that a book format allows.

Here you will find what can best be described as eulogies of learning, observations on that uniquely human endeavor we call education, and impassioned calls to see that endeavor in a new light. I have no doubt that it will inspire, not because of my words *per se*, but because of the light and life of students that, hopefully, shines through the essays. In fact, many of these pieces could be seen as effusive panegyrics, and if so, I am quite comfortable with that. I love my students, and if at times my words sound like the gushing praise of a parent, we should remember that *in loco parentis* is not merely a legal principle delineating a teacher's responsibilities. It also speaks to the heart of a role parents have graciously invited us to share with them.

This is your invitation to allow broad themes and high ideals to wash over you. This book is not about me or any particular pedagogical approaches I have used over the years. It is about truth, goodness, and beauty, especially as those are seen through the lives of students interacting with some of the greatest writings the world has known. By the end I hope you will have a clearer image when you hear words like "teaching," "school," or "education," one that is as sharp in your mind as the image you have upon hearing "golden waffle." And I hope that will lead you to understand why people once described education as a "grand object," and why some of us still do.

A Note on Style

As noted above, these essays were taken from my blog, yet there is a difference in the style of writing blog posts and composing essays. The former often contain attention-getting phrasing, eye-catching spacing and arrangement of text, and links to videos and other websites. When set in the format of a prose book, some of those features do not work well. In addition, blog posts that garner the most attention can be read on average in about seven minutes. With this book I have taken the opportunity to change some of the language to be more consistent with the essay format and have expanded ideas that needed clarification or invited additional thought.

I have taught at seven schools across my career. There was Martin Luther King, Jr. Latin Grammar Middle School in Kansas City, Missouri; The University of Texas, LBJ High School, and Austin Community College in Austin, Texas; North Central High School and Butler University in Indianapolis, Indiana; and St. Theodore Guerin Catholic High School in Noblesville, Indiana. Some of these essays make specific references to those schools, and although I considered removing those references to make the essays more generic, in the end I decided to keep them. The specificity of a place matters, and so it is important to know, for example, that MLK Latin Grammar Middle School was part of a magnet program in Kansas City to combat *de facto* segregation and that it was located just inside the 43rd Street Crip gang zone. It is important to know that North Central High School is one of the largest public high schools in Indiana and has a diverse enrollment of nearly four thousand students. It is important to know that Guerin Catholic is a small, private school of eight hundred students in which the Christian faith is foundational within the rigorous International Baccalaureate curriculum.

Finally, be warned that there are languages other than English in this book, most notably Latin and Greek. It is important for readers to have access to the original texts of quotations, even if they do not have a command of the languages in which they are written. Perhaps they will be inspired to study those languages or to seek a friend who knows them. Even if readers do neither of these, seeing words in a language other than one's own is an important reminder that theirs is not the only language in the world, and therefore theirs is not the only way of understanding things. I have provided translations for non-English passages. Unless otherwise noted, all translations are mine.

Philosophy and Education

I became acquainted with Sam Rocha through a mutual friend in 2013 and reviewed his book *A Primer for Philosophy and Education* in a series of posts in 2013 and 2014 that I have included here. Rocha is currently assistant professor in the Department of Educational Studies at The University of British Columbia in Vancouver. There are many books that are important in guiding our thinking about education, and I regret not being able to go into greater depth in this book about more of them. An unlikely one is *The Prince* by Machiavelli. A graduate student instructor of mine when I was an undergraduate at Indiana University, Hornfay Cherng, used it in one of our classes. He is now Director of the Master Program for Waldorf Teachers at National Tsing Hua University in Taiwan and cannot know how important his book choice was, for in addition to its excellent leadership advice, it showed me that a work intended for one purpose, *realpolitik* in the case of Machiavelli, can have other applications. There are, of course, classic works such as St. Augustine's *Against the Academicians* and the *Epistle on the Method of Study* by St. Thomas Aquinas, as well as numerous passages that touch on various aspects of learning scattered throughout the writings of the ancients. Among these, many of the epistles of Seneca are of great value to both educator and student alike. In more modern times we have the undeniable treasure of *The Idea of a University* (1873) by John Henry Newman, *Norms & Nobility* (1981) by David V. Hicks, and *Who Killed Homer?* (2001) by Victor Davis Hanson, to name only a few. One, however, deserves particular mention, and that is *Lessons of the Masters* by George Steiner. It should be required reading for anyone discerning the call to teach and merits frequent re-reading throughout a teacher's career.

Pieces of Advice

Some of the essays in this book could have been written at nearly any point in my career, but the presumption to give advice can only be made after significant experience. With more than thirty years of teaching at secondary and undergraduate levels, I have acquired the requisite experience, and whether that translates into worthwhile ideas, only others can say. The word "advice" itself is derived from Latin and ultimately means what seems to a person to be the case. In this section I share with fellow veteran teachers as well as with those who are new to the profession, administrators, and parents, what seem to me ideas and practices that can serve young people well in their educational endeavors. There are many other good ideas in the world that can help those who have any role to play in the nurture and development of young people. These just happen to be some of mine that I have collected while working with so many people in the noble endeavor of education. This will be the most practical part of this book, which is, by design, focused more on broad themes, high ideals, and abstract notions that can stir the soul.

If this seems like your cup of tea, then join me on the shared journey of discovery that is true education.

A Grand Object, or Pursuing the Greater Things

This book contains many ideas, but if there is one theme, it is that education is something far greater than offering someone a discrete piece of information. Too many students complain, perhaps not in these words, that they are inundated with discrete pieces of information and see no larger picture into which they all fit. They are left with the academic equivalent of the psychobilly Cadillac in Johnny Cash's 1976 song "One Piece at a Time," which tells the story of an automaker who slipped pieces of Cadillacs out of the factory in his lunchbox until he had enough to build a car. The problem was that the pieces ranged from the years 1949 through 1970, and when he attempted to assemble them, they did not fit together properly.

This is a common topic in discussions with teachers and those outside academic institutions who nevertheless have an interest in what transpires inside them, and the solution is quite simple even if it is not easy. Each teacher has some degree of autonomy over what takes place in his or her classroom. That autonomy is severely limited in some schools, but in none is it lacking entirely. Teachers have choices, and we must choose to pursue the greater things in our classes. We do this by first asking, "Greater than what?" This is then followed by the question, "What are those greater things?"

A perfectly satisfactory cake can come from a box with the directions printed on the side, but we all know that the most delicious treats are baked from family recipes passed down by word of mouth and committed more often to memory than to paper, and something similar is true regarding education. Teacher editions of textbooks and online lesson plans in the hands of someone who has been hired to do a job can lead to adequate understanding by students, but there is something much grander to be experienced by both students and teachers when the teacher goes beyond mere standards and objectives.

Many years ago, I was on a team that devised and delivered professional development related to the state standards in world language instruction. I pointed out that the standard was a variously decorated pole carried into battle by the ancient Roman soldiers. When the general gave orders to the standard bearer to move, the entire unit moved with him. The standard pointed the way, but it was never a goal beyond which no one was to move, and we used that metaphor as we presented the new academic standards around our state.

The grand object of a full education can be witnessed and felt, but it cannot be captured and contained in a spreadsheet. It cannot be limited by categories of evaluation or tasks to be checked off on a published curriculum. Simply put, there is more to it than that.

What, then, is that more? What are the greater things in second-grade spelling or sixth-grade math? What does going beyond the curriculum look like in eighth-grade science, sophomore English, or senior chemistry? I am a Latin teacher, and so you would need to ask teachers of other grades and subjects about their areas, but generally speaking, it means exploring the true, the good, and the beautiful in all things. Of course, teachers must search for those themselves in order to guide their students toward them, but these things, not instead of but alongside curriculum guides and standards, lead to the fullness that education can be.

Let us take as an example second-grade spelling. It is one thing to ask students to memorize a list of words. It is another to dazzle the minds of children by telling them that words, those squiggles on paper or those particular sounds that come from their mouths, are capable of carrying objects through time and space, for as Alfred Korzybski observed, words are time-binders.[1] Suppose for a moment that the word on the spelling list was "waffle." You pronounce the word in front of the class and write it in bold letters, then ask the students to draw a picture of what the word describes. After the students have produced their golden-brown masterpieces, you point out that merely by speaking the word "waffle" and writing it on the board, you were able to take an image from your own breakfast earlier that day and transport it into their minds. By introducing students to the idea that the two-syllable sound coming from their mouths or the six-letter word consisting of four consonants and two vowels on paper is an amazing construction called a time-binder, you have led them into deep, speculative waters. If this glimpse of the grand is possible in a second-grade spelling lesson, what grand things could students in other grades and classes come to see?

It is human nature to reach for the grand, which is why the framers of the original Indiana constitution chose it as the word they thought most appropriate when writing about education.[2] This natural tendency is perhaps best and most famously expressed in words from Robert Browning's poem "Andrea del Sarto,"

> Ah, but a man's reach should exceed his grasp,
> Or what's a heaven for?[3]

Yet it is equally the case that we can get our heads so lost in the stars that we stumble over what is in front of us. In his essay "On the education of children," Montaigne wrote, "[I]t is the achievement of a lofty and very strong soul to know how to come down to a childish gait and guide it. I walk more firmly and surely uphill than down."[4] Quite often teachers can become so intoxicated with heady notions of teaching critical thinking and helping students see bigger pictures that they fail to equip them to do those very things by passing over too quickly or entirely the foundations of a subject. Someone well versed in the Riemann hypothesis may understandably not wish to lead elementary students in a drill of multiplication facts. If a person cannot, as Montaigne put it, come down to a childish gait and guide it, then that person should not be a teacher in kindergarten through twelfth-grade classes. As in most things, balance is required, and while at times a class may need to tip more toward the end of mastering fundamentals and at others toward exploring grander themes, the challenge of the teacher is to be prepared for both as needed.

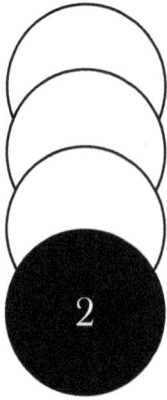

Plato and Back-to-School Night

Our second-year Latin students are studying Greek right now, both the language and the culture. Most educated Romans knew Greek, so it is fitting that our students get at least a passing familiarity with some of the highlights. After having studied the language a bit, they are now reading bits of Plato in translation, and we recently had a fascinating discussion of *Republic* V. The students were not surprisingly quite excited to learn that Plato advocated the same kind of education for women as for men. They were struck that someone from the 4th century B.C. could be so, as one student put it, "ahead of his time." And then we read this.

And this lawful use of them seems likely to be often needed in the regulations of marriages and births.

How so?

Why, I said, the principle has been already laid down that the best of either sex should be united with the best as often, and the inferior with the inferior, as seldom as possible; and that they should rear the offspring of the one sort of union, but not of the other, if the flock is to be maintained in first-rate condition. Now these goings on must be a secret which the rulers only know, or there will be a further danger of our herd, as the guardians may be termed, breaking out into rebellion.

Very true.

Had we not better appoint certain festivals at which we will bring together the brides and bridegrooms, and sacrifices will be offered and suitable hymeneal songs composed by our poets: the number of weddings is a matter which must be left to the discretion of the rulers, whose aim will be to preserve the average of the population? There are many other things which they will have to consider, such as the effects of wars and

diseases and any similar agencies, in order as far as this is possible to prevent the State from becoming either too large or too small.

Certainly, he replied.

We shall have to invent some ingenious kind of lots which the less worthy may draw on each occasion of our bringing them together, and then they will accuse their own ill-luck and not the rulers.

To be sure, he said.

And I think that our braver and better youth, besides their other honours and rewards, might have greater facilities of intercourse with the women given them; their bravery will be a reason, and such fathers ought to have as many sons as possible.

True.

And the proper officers, whether male or female or both, for offices are to be held by women as well as men –

Yes –

The proper officers will take the offspring of the good parents to the pen or fold, and there they will deposit them with certain nurses who dwell in a separate quarter; but the offspring of the inferior, or of the better when they chance to be deformed, will be put away in some mysterious, unknown place, as they should be.

Yes, he said, that must be done if the breed of the guardians is to be kept pure.

They will provide for their nurture, and will bring the mothers to the fold when they are full of milk, taking the greatest possible care that no mother recognizes her own child; and other wet-nurses may be engaged if more are required. Care will also be taken that the process of suckling shall not be protracted too long; and the mothers will have no getting up at night or other trouble, but will hand over all this sort of thing to the nurses and attendants.[5]

I am glad to say this section did not go over so well. One student pointed out that this was eugenics, and we talked about that. They observed that this was what the Nazis were after, and we talked about that. The students were bothered that the weaker offspring would be done away with, and we talked about that.

And then I pointed out that the treatment of the good offspring, i.e., being taken to a separate place in the city away from their parents and being reared by agents of the state, described their own situation. For indeed, what are public schools but places in the city, separate from students' homes, where children are taught by teachers who are agents of the state, paid via taxes?

This is where class became truly uncomfortable. The students did not like seeing their own situation described in the midst of a passage with which most people profoundly disagree. I was quick to point out that there can be things in a person's writings that we agree with and things that we do not. You take the good and toss the bad. Yet I also pointed out something else. I know some of my students' parents from back-to-school night and a few more from other interactions, but in general, parents entrust their children for the most productive hours of the day, five days a week, during the most formative years of their lives, to people they do not know.

It is true, of course, that teachers call home. We make ourselves available at back-to-school night. We reach out to our families. It is, however, vitally important that parents be involved in the lives of their children by knowing what is going on at their schools. They should know the names of their children's teachers, coaches, and principals. They should be as engaged as they can be in the life of the school. Admittedly, this takes on as many different appearances as there are families in a school. Some simply cannot be involved for any number of valid factors, and some take the easy way out.

Why did we read such a challenging passage in that class? We did so for many reasons, but perhaps chiefly for comments such as this. As they left my room, some of my students were making verbal recognition of the responsibility they would one day need to take in the lives of their own children.

Bloody Vengeance, or Why I Love High School

Education is a shared journey of discovery, and that was most evident one evening at North Central High School. One particular class of fifth-year Latin students, those who started Latin in eighth grade, spent most of their senior year exploring topics of particular interest to them. From philosophy to historical linguistics to bees...yes, bees...these intellectually curious and motivated students demonstrated the best in what we hope for from lifelong learners.

During the final quarter of the year, they decided to work together to look into something that few high school students even know exists, the tragedies of Seneca. Tradition says that Lucius Annaeus Seneca was born about 4 B.C., and despite his having once been the tutor of Nero, the emperor ordered him to commit suicide in A.D. 65. He is famous for his philosophical writings in Stoicism and his tragedies, which are decidedly not Stoic. To quote one of his modern translators, "Seneca's tragedies are intense. They show us people who push themselves too far, beyond the limits of ordinary behaviour and emotion. Passion is set against reason, and passion wins out.

Seneca's characters are obsessed and destroyed by their emotions: they are dominated by rage, ambition, lust, jealousy, desire, anger, grief, madness, and fear."[6]

Into this dark literary world that has influenced Elizabethan and Jacobean tragedy and has sparked almost unbroken interest for two millennia, a small group of Indiana high school seniors dared to enter. They read several of Seneca's works and settled on *Thyestes*, the revenge story that tells the tale of Atreus, father of Agamemnon and Menelaus of Trojan War fame, feeding to his brother Thyestes his brother's own children. They explored the vexed question of whether or not Seneca's plays were ever performed in antiquity and then set about the task of imagining how to perform this one in the 21st century. I should add that I had little to do with this. Other than providing some resources and asking questions, I left the students to their own devices. The result was the fulfillment of a dream for me.

On the night of their performance, a handful of parents and students gathered in a small auditorium at our school. The set and costuming were minimal by design, and for twenty-two minutes, four students presented their version of *Thyestes*, which drew heavily from the translation of Paul Murgatroyd. Immediately following the performance, we engaged in a time of questions and answers. We explored their choices in editing the play, their decisions regarding makeup, and whether or not there was any development or progression in the characters.

That explains the "bloody vengeance" in the title of this post, but what about the rest of it? I had long wanted to see high school students work with Seneca, but it just never happened. What the students in that class did was beyond my hopes, for they inspired me to think, and that is the reason for the second part of this essay's title. I simply love exploring the world and journeying with students on the quest for truth, goodness, and beauty. Does that sound a bit lofty? Perhaps it does, but then again, education is a lofty endeavor. High school students are curious without being jaded. What my students did with this play raised questions for me that I was eager to explore with students yet to come. I like to learn. I like to explore. I like to seek the answers to questions, and very often, my students are the ones who have inspired the most provocative ones.

As a result, I have been blessed to be able to pursue my own academic work as a high school teacher. Discussions with high school students have inspired me to publish articles on translation theory, Latin poetic composition, textual issues with Vergil's *Aeneid*, and the mind-body problem in philosophy. Without question, I would never have pursued these and other works were it not for my primary calling as a teacher, and for this reason I would encourage non-collegiate teachers to pursue their academic interests and creativity related to the subjects they teach. Publication and production within a certain discipline are not the prerogative alone of those who hold doctorate degrees.

Greek gives us the word *paidagogos* for "teacher," and Latin has *magister*, but they are not synonyms. The former literally means a leader of children, and the latter suggests a master of knowledge. Very often professional development for teachers focuses exclusively on pedagogy, or the art and practice of teaching. Yet teachers must display facets of both the *paidagogos* and the *magister*. It is crucial that the science teacher be involved in science, the art teacher be an artist, and that choir and orchestra teachers be musicians themselves. Someone who cooks from a recipe can prepare perfectly adequate meals, but a chef produces delight. When teachers allow themselves to be inspired by what happens in the classroom to pursue related matters of scholarship or creativity outside the classroom, the result is that the classroom becomes an even richer place for everyone.

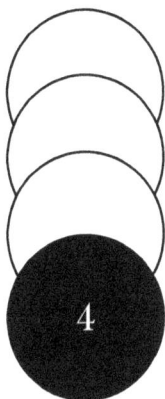

A Tale of Two Schools

In the movie *Tin Cup*, a down-on-his-luck driving range operator (Kevin Costner) instructs a psychiatrist (Rene Russo) to hit a golf ball. He waxes a bit poetic as he models the swing while describing it. "I think of the golf swing as a poem," says Roy "Tin Cup" McAvoy. "The opening phrase of this poem will always be the grip. The hands unite to form a single unit by the simple overlap of the little finger. Lowly and slowly the club head is led back, pulled into position not by the hands but the body, which turns away from the target, shifting weight to the right side without shifting balance. Tempo is everything, perfection unattainable, as at the top of the swing there's a hesitation, a little nod to the gods...that he is fallible, that perfection is unattainable. Weight shifts to the left pulled by the powers in the earth. It's alive, this swing, a living sculpture, and down through contact, striking the ball crisply, with character."

Anyone who has ever attempted to play golf has probably heard the litany of things that must be done to launch a tiny, white ball away from you just so you can walk to find it and hit it again. Overlap your fingers. The V formed by the thumb and forefinger should be pointed over your shoulder. Keep your left arm straight. Don't break your wrists. Keep the club parallel to the ground on the takeaway. Turn your torso and shift your weight, but do not move laterally. Keep your head still. Swing down and through the ball. And of course, the cardinal rule, keep your eye on the ball.

With these and countless other tips running through your head as you stand on the tee box preparing to expose yourself as never before in front of God and all the world, it is a wonder we do not all fall into a fetal position, tearfully sucking our thumbs. I have no doubt that some have.

How close is this to a teacher's daily life? Align your lessons to state standards. Adhere to the school grading policy. Follow best practices. Prepare for the test. Don't teach to the test. Incorporate technology. Know the learning styles of each student. Incorporate the learning styles of each student. Be familiar with educational acronyms and abbreviations. Utilize the concepts the acronyms and abbreviations stand for. Continue to develop your skills with professional development. Stay on top of your content.

As with the received wisdom on how to swing a golf club, the thoughts that crowd a teacher's mind are not all bad. Some may even be good. Yet when the mind is thus inundated as teachers stand before their classes preparing to expose themselves in front of God and all the world, it is a wonder they do not run screaming from the profession. I know for a fact that some have.

Kevin Costner does offer one other approach. He tells Rene Russo, clearly overwhelmed by the poetic physics of it all, "There's only one other acceptable theory about how to hit the ball. Grip it and rip it."

I am certainly not suggesting that teachers can enter a classroom with no thought or preparation for how to lead students and guide them toward understanding. I am saying that there is simply too much in education right now. There are too many mandates, requirements, suggestions, theories, ideas, tips, strategies, rules, procedures. There is too much riding on what does not matter and too little riding on what does. Any sane person, out of sheer necessity, has learned to ignore much of the blooming, buzzing confusion. We must step back from it all, at least every once in a while, and just grip it and rip it. We must ignore the clamor and do what we know, deep in our souls, to do. Will we make mistakes? We certainly will. Is it possible a student will not learn something he or she should because of a mistake we have made? Yes, and it is not the end of the world. If we can work with each other in genuine collegiality and not through a forced meeting or structure imposed upon us from above, we can recover from our mistakes and become even better.

Later in the movie, Kevin Costner's swing falls apart. He loses his touch. His friend, played by Cheech Marin, spends hours on the driving range analyzing his swing, but all the theories and rules fail to restore Costner's ability. Eventually, Marin changes tactics. "Take all your change and put it in your left-hand pocket. All right, now tie your left shoe in a double knot. Turn your hat around backwards. Now take this tee and stick it behind your left ear."

Costner takes a sweet swing and sends the ball far down range. Stunned, he asks Marin how he had been able to hit such a great shot.

"Because you're not thinking about shanking. You're not thinking, period. You're just lookin' like a fool and hittin' the ball pure and simple. Your brain was getting in the way."

My ideas for education reform will not draw big bucks. They are not data driven. I am simply suggesting that from time to time we get back to the human aspect of this most human enterprise called education. Sometimes we need to risk looking like fools. We need to turn off the sound and fury of the educational world and, pedagogically speaking, grip it and rip it.

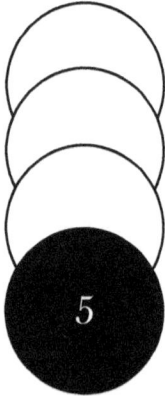

Icing On the Cake

What do you love most about teaching? As much as I love a scintillating conversation with engaged students about Latin grammar, Greek philosophy, Ciceronian oratory, or Vergilian poetry, the over-the-top-blow-my-mind-make-my-heart-swell-to-the-point-it-will-explode thrill for me is telling parents the amazing things I see in their children.

Last night was our annual Latin Club awards dinner. On the surface, it was a humble, albeit large, affair. One hundred forty students, parents, and siblings met in our school's cafeteria for pizza and pop. It was not exactly *haute cuisine*, but food was not our focus. We assembled so that once again I could distribute seemingly endless local, state, and national awards that our students had won for their work in academics, art, and dramatic competitions, all related to the languages and cultures of ancient Greece and Rome.

Yet for all the pyrotechnic honors of the National Latin Exam and the National Junior Classical League Latin Honor Society, the thrill beyond compare for me was in talking directly with parents. When I tell parents how much I have enjoyed having their son or daughter in class, what extraordinary contributions he or she has made to class discussions, or how I see leadership qualities developing in him or her, I see a sparkle in their eyes. It is the sparkle of appreciation that someone outside their family sees what they see. It is the sparkle of surprise that someone outside their family sees what they have never seen. It is the sparkle that represents what they and I both feel toward these amazing young people...love.

What are the other highlights of the school year for me? There is back-to-school night. Yes, it makes for a long day, but I absolutely love meeting parents and sharing with them all the things their children have already been doing and the prospects for the year ahead. There are also letters of recommendation, of which I have written hundreds for jobs, scholarships, and university placements. I have the inestimable privilege of putting on paper the phenomenal achievements and qualities that I have seen developing in the young people who will lead the world. What is the unifying factor in all of these? It is the opportunity to share with others the amazing, extraordinary, breathtaking abilities and, even more importantly, character, of the young people with whom I am blessed to spend my working life.

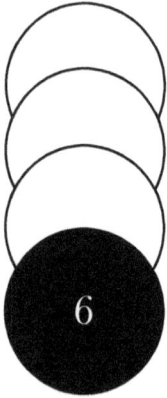

Getting Off Track

We are behind in our Advanced Placement Latin class, which is a typical condition for us. In fact, we frequently joke that at first we get behind, then behinder, then behindest, and finally we end up the most behindest of all. There are certain lines we must cover, certain concepts we must explore, and as it was last Friday, certain grammatical concepts we must review. Yet for all that, we are reading Vergil's *Aeneid*, an epic poem the depths of which I have not yet discovered, despite having taught it for longer than my students have been alive. It is a *magnum opus* dealing with love and hate, life and death, dreams inspired and hopes crushed. It is, as with most Roman art, a distinctly human work. Do you think for one minute that with such a work in the hands of thoughtful young people about to launch into the epic of their own lives I would not indulge their thought-provoking questions just to stay on the syllabus? Not on your life.

We were at Book I, line 521, in which the hero Aeneas catches sight of a friend, whom he believed dead, about to speak to a foreign queen. Of this man Vergil writes, "*Maximus Ilioneus placido sic pectore coepit.*" "Ilioneus, the greatest of them all, began to speak thus with a calm heart." Nick, a football and rugby player with a Shakespearean vocabulary and the poetic soul of Shelley, observed that *pectore* also means "chest," and thus began our discussion of why the word can mean "heart" as well. Will, a young man also studying for the International Baccalaureate exam in Latin, then asked why Vergil would have referenced the heart as the seat of emotions, since there is evidence the ancients saw the liver as our emotional source. This gave me pause, as I did not at the moment recall that the origin of this notion lay with Galen, who lived more than a century after Vergil. We reflected on the parallel expression Vergil likes to use, *ex imo corde*, "from the depths of the heart," which uses the word for the actual heart muscle. The conversation flitted from student to student, and then I paused again and uttered a statement that made all heads turn.

"This is why I do not like tests."

I explained that in our current obsession with using methodology from the natural sciences to assess the value of what takes place in this most human of enterprises, education, our tools are incapable of capturing the truth. What test could I give that would accurately take stock of the scintillating discussion that had taken place over the previous fifteen minutes? We could count the number of students who actually spoke during that time, but if we did that, then the conclusion would be that the exercise was a disastrous failure, for fewer than fifty percent had spoken. Jess, a thoughtful young lady, observed, "Yes, but everyone was thinking." Of that, I have no doubt, but I do doubt that any of the Olympian powers-that-be in education would accept sparkles in teenage eyes or pensive expressions as data.

Yong Zhao, internationally renowned scholar, author, and speaker on education, wrote once about our suicidal obsession with attaining educational excellence through authoritarian means.[7] He is right, but since education is a human endeavor, conducted by people with people about the discoveries and creations of people, it must be about life, and I cannot go down the path of death, even if it were to lead to 5s for everyone on the A.P. exam. My student Jess said it best at the end of the period. As the bell rang to dismiss our class, the next to last of the day, which was a Friday and a day when many expect schools to get little of value accomplished, she stayed to say thank you. She thanked me for allowing our class to get off track and to discuss matters that truly matter.

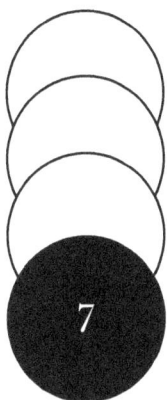

You Hold the Heavens in Your Head

When apparently the last eminent guest had long ago taken his place, again those three bugle-blasts rang out, and once more the swords leaped from their scabbards. Who might this late comer be? Nobody was interested to inquire. Still, indolent eyes were turned toward the distant entrance, and we saw the silken gleam and the lifted sword of a guard of honor plowing through the remote crowds. Then we saw that end of the house rising to its feet; saw it rise abreast the advancing guard all along like a wave. This supreme honor had been offered to no one before. There was an excited whisper at our table – 'Mommsen!' – and the whole house rose – rose and shouted and stamped and clapped and banged the beer-mugs. Just simply a storm! Then the little man with his long hair and Emersonian face edged his way past us and took his seat. I could have touched him with my hand – Mommsen! – think of it!

I would have walked a great many miles to get a sight of him, and here he was, without trouble, or tramp, or cost of any kind. Here he was, clothed in a titanic deceptive modesty which made him look like other men. Here he was, carrying the Roman world and all the Caesars in his hospitable skull, and doing it as easily as the other luminous vault, and the skull of the universe, carries the Milky Way and the constellations.[8]

During the winter of 1891-1892, Mark Twain was in Berlin and attended a celebration for scientists Rudolf Virchow and Hermann von Helmholtz. The passage above is Twain's description of what happened when Classics scholar Theodor Mommsen entered the room, and I was thinking of this story as I sat on the Tarmac of the Newark airport after a three-day conference of Teachers of the Year in Princeton. I had begun reading an article in the journal *The Classical Outlook* on the comparison between Ulysses Grant's *Memoirs* and Caesar's *Commentaries on the Gallic War*. A quotation from Twain prompted memory of the Mommsen story, and with it came the thrill of academic remembrance, of being able to make connections, to say "this is that."

And then the nagging thought came of whether any of this mattered. I had a moment of thrill as I read an academic article on an airplane, a moment unlikely to have been shared with another living soul. I know many such moments, and while I am blessed to have family and friends with whom I can share them, I obviously do not share them all. There are thoughts, connections, realizations that exist only in my head and that will go with me to the grave.

This is not a morbid meditation, for it prompted me to think that the same is true for the baggage handler on the ground, all the other passengers on board, and you. Whoever you are, you carry infinity within the stone boundaries of your skull. Memories and connections and ideas and speculations and questions and answers the smallest fraction of which will be known to none other than you form the vast cosmos of your experience. Infinity is sitting next to me in 6-C reading a newspaper. The universe is in the car ahead of you at the stoplight.

And we are tiny. Oh, yes, we are small. We are five feet tall on average, weigh a hundred odd pounds, and can fit the infinity house of our heads inside a baseball cap. And there are millions, billions of us all over a planet that is but one point of light in the night sky.

What amazing, extraordinary creatures we are, what vastly interesting beings in a complex and fantastic world that beggars the description of any author! Savoring this, tasting it, exploring it, plunging head first into it...this is life. It is also why I am a teacher.

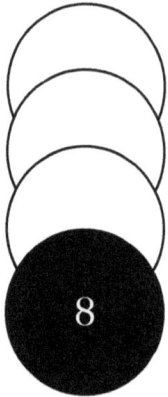

Impetus of the Undistinguished Host

8

In 1913-1914, Sir Arthur Quiller-Couch delivered a series of lectures at Cambridge that were collected into a book titled *On the Art of Writing*. It is a book in which I have highlighted more passages than not, and one of those passages seems to speak especially to our present age. In his second lecture, he advocates the writing of poetry among university students in addition to their reading and studying of it. "Recollect that in Poesy as in every other human business, the more there are who practice it the greater will be the chance of *someone's* reaching perfection. It is the impetus of the undistinguished host that flings forward a Diomed or a Hector."

What does this mean? It means quite simply that we will never know whether the next Homer or Einstein is sitting in our classes unless we expose the greatest number of students to the widest possible curriculum. Put another way, students cannot exercise genius in a field they do not even know exists.

It also acknowledges the truth that not everyone will be such a genius. Thousands of warriors fought in the Trojan War, yet literature and art commemorate only a few, such as Diomedes and Hector. An Einsteinian level of achievement by every student in the class is an absurd goal, and its failure of attainment is no argument against offering the class in the first place. Not everyone needs to achieve the level of the hero or the genius, but if anyone is to have any hope of doing so, then the opportunity must be placed before all.

This is why each school must offer the widest possible curriculum to its students. Art is on an equal footing with math, Latin with physics, and physical education with the Advanced Placement or International Baccalaureate class. To cut one for the sake of another is to decide out of hand that no students will achieve great things in a particular subject.

Quiller-Couch also exposed a dishonoring truth in British life that shames America today. "We may prate of democracy, but actually a poor child in England has little more hope than had the son of an Athenian slave to be emancipated into that intellectual freedom of which great writings are born." Is this really so different one hundred years and an ocean away? Citizens of the United States have the money to afford whatever sort of education we want. In 2022 people in the United States spent $60.46 billion in casinos, $107.92 billion on lottery tickets, and $259.8 billion on alcohol. By the end of 2023, we had spent almost $50 billion on chocolate, which does not take into account other types of candy.[9] Homer and Einstein may be sitting in a class near you. Is it worth it to us to find out?

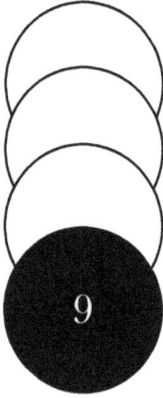

Ancient Efficiency Expert Speaks to Modern Students

It was a two-hour snow delay, so we did not have much time in each class. Yet as our second-year Latin classes began their reading of the Roman historian Livy, I could not help taking some time to explore a life lesson.

Livy wrote of an event during the reign of Tullus Hostilius, who ruled as Rome's third king between 673 and 642 B.C. Rome was at war with Alba Longa, and as there was a set of triplet brothers in each army, the kings decided to allow the two sets of triplets to fight, with the winning side declaring victory in the war.

Right away two of the Roman triplets were killed, and all three of the Albans sustained wounds. The one surviving Roman, who was unhurt, now faced a choice. These are Livy's words.

Ut universis solus nequaquam par, sic adversus singulos ferox.[10]

"Just as alone he was in no way equal to all of them, so against them individually he was fierce."

On a day when we really did not have time for a digression, we digressed. We discussed the insanely busy lives of American students, who take a heavy load of classes that are followed by extra-curricular activities, sports, jobs, and home responsibilities, to say nothing of emotional and relational challenges common to their age and often the physical challenges of poverty that should be common to none. I pointed out that, similar to the Roman hero of the story, they were not equal to all the tasks of their lives at once, but that against them individually, they could be fierce. We talked about the overwhelming sensation of facing a mountain of homework, but that setting a time limit for each assignment and working only on that, taking a short break, and moving on to the next was a better way to approach the whole.

We continued our reading to see that the Roman, Horatius, turned from his three wounded enemies and began to run. The Romans thought he was fleeing, but as Horatius looked over his shoulder, he saw that the three wounded Albans were pursuing him at great intervals, with the most severely wounded bringing up the rear. Suddenly, he turned and attacked the one who was closest to him.

We digressed again.

What was the condition of the Alban in closest pursuit to the Roman? The students easily observed that he would have been the least wounded. As Horatius fought each of the three Albans, which fight would have been the most difficult? Again, they quickly noted that the first would have been most challenging, as that opponent was the least wounded and therefore the strongest of his brothers.

We then talked about the value of approaching the most difficult assignments first. It is natural to want to put those off to the end, but far better to approach those first when minds are fresh, leaving shorter or easier assignments to the end.

I have my doubts regarding what those students will remember about Latin grammar over the years, and perhaps they will soon forget the story of triplet brothers as well, but if they remember anything, I hope it is the application of an ancient war story to the busyness of modern life. If they do, then our class period, although reduced in time, was expanded in effect.

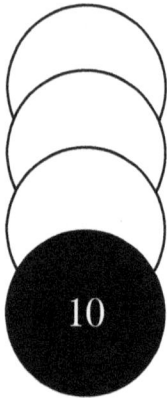

Drink Deep, or Taste Not

10

A little learning is a dang'rous thing.
Drink deep, or taste not the Pierian spring.
There shallow draughts intoxicate the brain,
And drinking largely sobers us again.

"Essay on Criticism," lines 215-218, Alexander Pope

While some would take Pasteur's famous dictum that "chance favors the prepared mind" to be a defense of the well-structured lesson plan, I argue that we must be careful not to get lost in the details. Am I prepared to teach my classes? I am—in that I know my subject matter extremely well and understand how teenage students learn best. Do I walk into a class with everything scripted? God forbid.

Take a recent Advanced Placement Latin class. We were reading the scene in *Aeneid*, Book VI, in which the hero, Aeneas, enters the underworld. Vergil describes the Styx, a river on which the gods trembled to take an oath.

He talks of the souls that had to wander its banks for a hundred years because their bodies had not been buried. All of this prompted questions from the students. What would happen if the gods swore by the Styx, yet broke their promise? If someone died by being eaten by a lion, would that count as burial, or would the person have to wait until the lion died and was buried?

We discussed why questions like these are often asked by those who are used to consulting a sacred text on such matters. Look it up in the Bible or in the Qur'an, we say. Such textual authority for what amounts to rather legalistic questions, however, just does not exist with regard to Greco-Roman mythology. Yet I began to wonder. To what extent was logical or philosophical or theological thought brought to bear on the Greco-Roman divinities and their interaction with the world? Was there any sort of systematic theology relative to Greco-Roman myth?

So, I asked. I asked friends of mine, including Joe Day (professor emeritus of Classics at Wabash College), Stephanie Larson (professor of Classics at Bucknell University), and Betty Rose Nagle (then professor of Classical Studies at Indiana University). I immediately got back responses. I received a discussion on "efforts to organize what was, in religious reality, a vast polytheistic, localist non-system into a more or less coherent system or pantheon" by the likes of Homer and Hesiod and a link to the writings of Xenophon against the traditional Homeric and Hesiodic portrayal. I even got an answer to what would happen if the gods did not keep their Styx-bound word. They would suffer ten years of death-like suspended animation.

And then I took that back to the classroom where my students and I spent a bit of time talking about ancient theology before progressing with the Vergil text.

This is education at its finest. It is, as I have so often described it, a shared journey of discovery. My students asked questions that turned me into a student again, and so I took those questions to other teachers and returned with answers to my own students. I have read the *Aeneid* countless times, yet every time I read it with students it is new as we explore together the mysteries and glories of the world.

11 A Teacher's Natural Habitat

There is a natural habitat for a teacher. It is a "sound and sweet and wise place" that is "surrounded by beauty and sanity," a place where "the whole human being, not disembodied chunks of him, is the focus of education."

And what may teachers expect in their natural habitat? They should expect "the joy of teaching" and perhaps even a certain "happy boyish enthusiasm" as "souls [are] born in wonder." They can expect "cheerful faces, and plenty of them" and "happy students" who are "not eager to leave, because they [are] having too much fun."

You will likely have one of two reactions to such a description of the teacher's natural habitat. You may sit back and sigh with a faraway look of longing as your heart yearns for such an Eden. You may also find a certain anger rising within you, a burning, righteous indignation that someone would even dare to describe a place that is so far from your present circumstance that it could not be glimpsed with the Hubble.

I know both of those reactions, but I also know that the descriptions offered above are about what should be, what can be, and what - in some places - actually is. These descriptions come from two articles, one about[11] and one by Anthony Esolen.[12] Tony Esolen was a tenured professor of literature at Providence College in Rhode Island before moving, after decades at that institution, to Thomas More College in New Hampshire. In addition to being a teacher of literature, he is also a poet, an acute critic of contemporary culture, and a translator, perhaps most notably of Dante. I have read him for years and can say only this. If you see his name on it, read it.

From the kindergarten teacher to the dissertation supervisor, any teacher who has spent more than one year in this calling has known the joy of teaching that he describes. They have known it at least once, or they would not have returned.

In the article by Esolen, he writes, "Then came the joy of teaching. I'm a born teacher. I don't mean to say that I am great at it—I'm quite aware of my flaws, which I'd rather not enumerate. I mean that even when I was a little boy I wanted to show people things, just because I liked them and wanted to share them. Teaching, for me, has always retained much of that happy boyish enthusiasm; it's why I find it hard to understand people who turn teaching into politics by other means."[13]

This is what teaching is...raw, unbounded, childlike enthusiasm. And if something like justice should come from it because it has been about the work of the true, the good, and the beautiful, then so much the better, but teaching is not first and foremost about justice or someone's finding a job or gaining a credential. It is not, as Tony Esolen puts it, politics by other means. It is something much grander than that, taking in far more territory, and, when it is allowed to flourish in its natural habitat, it produces a harvest of many of the best things known to man.

And then in that same article he writes of one group of his students, "They were not eager to leave, because they were having too much fun. They were having too much fun—repeat this sentence three times carefully— reading Virgil in Latin, with a gray-haired fellow they had never met before. I drove home almost in tears."

This is a joy like no other, and I have been blessed to taste it. Teenagers in a last period class on a Friday, deeply engrossed in their Latin and asking questions and contributing meaningfully to the great conversation is what education can be, and we must fight each and every effort to turn education, which, because it is a supremely human endeavor must be characterized by life, into a zombie, the walking dead version of its true self.

So where is this blessed abode of teachers, this Elysium of education? Some teachers find it by carving it out of the blackboard jungle in which they find themselves. They must make bricks without straw as they guide and shape minds all while trying to turn their own schools into suitable learning environments. This, however, is not as it should be, and while decent-minded folk rightly laud their efforts, families of students and the citizenry at large should never for one moment think that this is good. Teachers should not have to fight those both inside and outside their profession to make their schools what they ought to be.

There are also those who leave a toxic environment for one in which their teaching arts can be given full expression. Esolen himself is in this category, and it would be pharisaical in the extreme to fault him for it. He writes, "Sometimes a single encounter with what is healthy and *ordinary*—I use the word advisedly, with its suggestion that things are in the order that God by means of his handmaid Nature has ordained—is enough to shake you out of the bad dreams of disease and confusion." By contrast he observes, "I came home recently from a day at Thomas More College, full of good cheer and energy, and for somebody who isn't getting younger, those can take you a long way. They can add many years to your life as a teacher, whereas discouragement and disappointment lead to exhaustion."

I can only add my affirmation to this, for I, too, have known the exhausting discouragement and disappointment when a school was not what it should be. More importantly, however, I have known the vital enthusiasm that comes from educational environments that are healthy, and when these are ordinary in the sense Esolen suggests, the teacher's habitat is a paradise indeed.

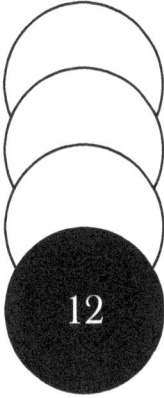

12 On Handwriting and More

Tucked away inside a Master's thesis from over a half century ago lies the kind of broad thinking that once characterized American education. Make no mistake, the thesis is filled with the sort of data reporting one would expect after reading its title, "An Evaluation of Two Methods of Teaching Handwriting: a seminar report submitted in partial fulfillment of the requirements for a Master's Degree in the Department of Education, July 28, 1964." There are discussions of methods, reviews of relevant literature, and tables of results from a study conducted among fourth graders from February 12 to May 8, 1964, at Mt. Tabor Elementary School in New Albany, Indiana. Yet on three pages in the middle of the thesis, its author looks up from her research to find a larger view.

[L]anguage is the chief factor in the development of the human mind and civilization. It is what chiefly raises man above animal. The discovery of written language marked a great advance in the life of mankind since it made possible wider communication and more permanent records. This, in turn, made possible the accumulation of knowledge and the growth of literature, history, and science.

The individual child profits from the possession of the reading matter which has thus been produced. He also profits from his own acquisition of the ability to write. It, of course, gives him a means of communicating in addition to oral speech, but this is not all. In speech, the words disappear into thin air as they are spoken. They make a momentary impression and then they are gone. The form and structure of the sentences, paragraphs, and larger units cannot well be comprehended and criticized. Their logic cannot readily be grasped or their fallacies noted. They are heard one after the other, but they cannot be seen simultaneously so that their relation may be readily recognized. Francis Bacon expressed something of this idea when he said, "Reading maketh a full man, conference a ready man, and writing an exact man." Writing, then, is not merely a utilitarian art; it is a vital factor in the child's intellectual growth. (p. 34)

The author of this thesis, a 27-year-old teacher in her fifth year of teaching, knew that the teaching of handwriting was about far more than skills training. She understood it, rightly, as equipping children to take their place within the grand human story, one that involves not only their reading of literature, history, and science, but their contribution to such fields as well.   Yet even work within literature, history, and science can be little more than utilitarian endeavors, and this is especially the case when such work is evaluated only for its immediate result. The author of this thesis saw something deeper here, too.

Character development can be a by-product of every subject taught. Habits of physical and mental self-control, promptness, industry, self-reliance, a sense of neatness, pride in work well-done, exactness, tenacity, and perseverance might all grow out of the teaching of handwriting. (pp. 37-38)

Character development can be a by-product of every subject taught. It can be, but it only will be when teachers and education leaders look up from the utilitarian and immediately practical, from the evaluation of charts and data, and from the narrow focus that is blinding too many of us. It can be, but it only will be when we, like this young Master's student, who happened to be my mother, return to the broad thinking and larger view that helped American education produce some of the greatest thinkers, innovators, and leaders in history.

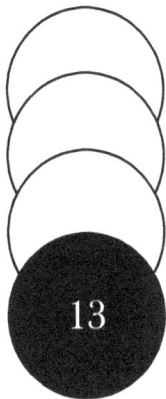

When a Student Asks a Question

The school district in which I have been teaching for many years once allowed eighth grade students to begin their world language study at the high school. Although that opportunity has been cut, we still have a few fifth-year students who began their Latin studies earlier than most, and this allows them to explore areas of academic interest outside the traditional curricula in first-year through fourth-year Latin.

One of those students recently asked me if I had any Plato in the room, and this confused me, since I had tasked them with deciding on something to read in Latin. He went on to explain that he wanted a Latin translation of Plato, and I paused. I could think of no Latin translations of Plato, despite that the ancient Romans certainly knew his works, and so I told my student I would have to get back with him.

During my prep period I did a bit of research and found an article that explained why I could think of no Latin versions of Plato. In his article "Two Thousand Years of Latin Translation from the Greek," Dean Lockwood observed that not only was there little need for translation since most educated Romans knew Greek, but also the Romans went in more for imitation and adaptation than straight translation. Plautus and Terence wrote their own plays, Cicero and Seneca developed their own philosophies, and Horace and Vergil composed their own poetry, and while all of these were heavily influenced by Greek originals, it was translation by way of adaptation rather than literal translation in which the Romans were most engaged.[14]

This was interesting enough, and I quickly printed the article to share with the students later in the day, but I had also run across references to Renaissance Latin translations of Plato, and this made me curious to find a text online. I soon found two sources for Marsilio Ficino's *Platonis Opera Omnia*, which was originally published in the 1480s.[15]

I quickly printed the first two pages of *Republic*, Book 7, which my students had read in translation during a Greek unit in second-year Latin, and at that point I began wishing the hours away until the last period of the day when I would see these students. In the meantime, I asked my department chair if she would like to sit in on that period, for I would have something exciting to share.

When the last period of the day finally rolled around, I instructed the third- and fourth-year Latin students on what to work on and then met with the fifth-year Latin students and my department chair. I was like a kid at Christmas! We discussed the Lockwood article and why it made sense that the ancient Romans would not have produced a translation of Plato. We then explored the Ficino translation, observing the difficulty of reading the typeface with its ligatures and abbreviations that were holdovers from calligraphy of the manuscript days, but noting also the relatively easy reading of the Latin itself.

In the end, the students decided to read some of the Roman philosophy of Seneca and Cicero because the typeface of modern editions is easier to see, but they agreed that it was fascinating to explore this Renaissance work and to marvel at what is available to us through digitized editions of works that would otherwise rarely see the light of day.

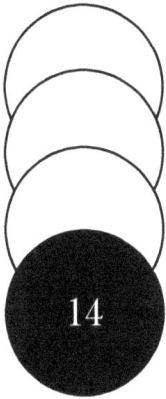

Making a Teacher Cry

14

Any number of things can make me cry while teaching, although I try to hide it the best I can. More often than not, it is the depth of insight from one of my students that so unsettles me. It is rather like snapping one's head to look at a brilliant work of art or to hear a bit of sublime music while walking through the humdrum of the day, lost in a sea of less important details. This time it happened during the last period of the day.

It was my Advanced Placement Latin class, and before you make assumptions about my students or our school, you should know that my school at the time was a large, midwestern, public high school with an enrollment between three and four thousand students. This particular class was evenly split between boys and girls and was ethnically diverse. As you read the rest of this story, do not assume it was set in an ivory tower.

Class started with a discussion of accents, what connotations are associated with them, and whether those same connotations exist for all people. Do the flowing vowel sounds of Italian or the sharp consonants of German produce the same effects in you as they do in me? Do they conjure the same feelings in other non-Italian- or non-German-speaking people as they do in many

English speakers?

It was an all-virtual class, and one of the benefits was the private chat function. Not a day passed when at least one student in nearly every class did not message me privately a question or comment I could address with the whole class without revealing that student's name. It was a help like no other for quiet students and those who like to think more deeply before they speak.

In this particular A.P. Latin class during the last period of the day, one of my students texted the following in response to our discussion about accents. "The best way to tell the beauty of an accent is if it enthralls you, even if you don't understand a word." This time I did a horrible job of hiding my tears. When I shared the comment aloud, others commented that we had a true wordsmith or even a Shakespeare among us.

Just as I had no time to ponder the depth of that comment or the beauty of its expression in the moment, I will leave you no time to do so, but will move on to what happened next. As you read, let these powerful moments build up and wash over you.

From there, we dove into our text, starting at *Aeneid* I.561. As we read the line, "*Tum breviter Dido vultum demissa profatur*," I had to stop to share with them something that had occurred earlier in the day during my third-year Latin class. That class had been reading Sallust's *Bellum Catilinae* and were at the part where Catiline, the infamous conspirator of the late first century B.C., prepared to address the senate *demisso voltu*. Even people without Latin can pick out the two similar phrases, *vultum demissa* in Vergil and demisso voltu in Sallust. I pointed out that both expressions contain the same words and mean the same thing, "with a downcast expression," but that they used different grammatical structures. Vergil opted for a purely adjectival function of the participle *demissa* and an accusative form of *vultum* expressing respect. The character Dido was literally downcast with respect to her face. Sallust, on the other hand, had put both words into the ablative case, using an incredibly common construction known as the ablative absolute.

One of my students asked what, if anything, was being conveyed by Vergil's grammatical choice, and I pointed out that it was in clear imitation of Greek, for Greek likes to use the accusative of respect. My student pressed on to ask why he would do that, and this led us to a brief discussion of the King

James translation of the Bible. One of the notable features of that translation, itself drawing heavily on previous English versions, was its casting of certain Hebraisms into English. For example, where English might more readily say, "God's son," the King James translators used "son of God," for the pattern "X of Y" is common in Hebrew. In a similar way, I explained, Vergil clearly imitated Homer without slavishly aping him, and this connected his new epic with the Homeric works from a millennium prior.

Still without time to pause, I had to end that session with my fourth-year Advanced Placement Latin students and switch over to a breakout room online where my fifth-year Latin students were deciding what they wanted to study next. At that particular school, fifth-year Latin provided a rare opportunity for students to explore topics of interest, and as we were starting a new quarter, it was time to see where they wanted to go. One student began by saying she had been reading recently about rhetorical and logical fallacies. I nearly stumbled going to the board to write down her ideas and asked if she were reading such things for a class. She said she was not, but had been inspired by other classes to look into those topics. She thought she might want to pursue something with logic, rhetoric, or philosophy in her next Latin project. Another student said she wanted to revisit some medieval studies we had pursued in third-year Latin, and another talked of exploring medical topics, including mental health issues and the quality of life for women in ancient Rome.

Now you can pause to consider what you have just read. These were utterly extraordinary, ordinary students. They were perfectly ordinary in that they, like the rest of their peers, followed fashion trends and enjoyed popular entertainment. They cared about their friends and about what people thought of them. They were simultaneously excited and apprehensive about college and they loved to goof around. Yet they were extraordinary in the depth of their curiosity and willingness to pursue it. And I would argue that what made them extraordinary could well be experienced by many more their age. Depth, breadth, curiosity, eloquence...these are not the things of the rare few, but are the gems common to the human treasury, and when my students hold them up to the light, the sparkle quite often brings a tear to my eyes.

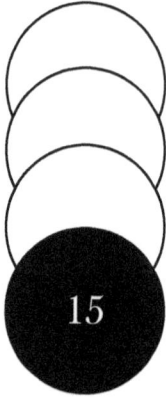

We Don't Always Need to Teach

15

"In Greece there are most lovely wild flowers. They would be beautiful anywhere, but Greece is not a rich and fertile country of wide meadows and fruitful fields where flowers seem at home. It is a land of rocky ways and stony hills and rugged mountains, and in such places the exquisite vivid bloom of wild flowers comes as a startling surprise."[16]

This is the passage that a high school junior who is the student of a friend of mine chose for a typical read-and-respond assignment. What that student wrote regarding this quotation forms a powerful reminder, or perhaps a startlingly new idea, that all teachers would do well to bear in mind.

"I personally enjoyed this quote because it was so vivid in details that I could visualize what was being described. This quote struck me because it was not about something that could be taught or learned and applied to one's life. It is simply a quote describing details of Greece. I think it is important to also recognize quotes or passages like this one because sometimes in life we need the simpler things rather than always looking at quotes that are about how we should live our lives, passages that teach. Yes, teaching and guidance quotes and passages are good but so are the descriptive ones, the ones that transport us into a space in our minds that is purely creative and imaginative. Quotes like this one...make whatever the reader is reading far more interesting because quotes like this allow that reader to imagine what ancient Greece or any other place from the past would have been like. This may be a simple quote, but I see something deeper in this quote that is very important.... It brings out the creative and imaginative side of literature."

We sometimes think of lyric poetry in classical literature as being that which does not advance the plot. It is personal and emotional. It sets up mood and atmosphere and evokes feelings. When, for example, the Roman poet Catullus in his fifth poem asks of his beloved, "Give me a thousand kisses and then a hundred more/And then another thousand and a hundred like before/Then add another thousand and a hundred to the score," he could have more simply said, "Give me 3,300 kisses." Yet, as Howard Nemerov so elegantly put it, there is a line between prose and poetry like that between rain and snow.[17] It is as indiscernible as the moment of transition from rain to snow, but it exists and it is the realm of lyric, and to be honest, would you not much rather have your lover propose passion in the lyrical way of Catullus than with a prosaic, mathematical sum?

And this brings us back to what this high school student observed and that teachers should remember. Education is not always about teaching and learning facts. It is not always about producing something with those learned facts, whether on a test or through a project or presentation. It is not, as it were, always about advancing the plot. There is a necessarily lyrical aspect to education as well.

We seem to have lost sight of this, and there can be no more unfortunate or compelling proof than in the numbers of students who have told me over the years that they have lost their love of reading because of their English classes. I enjoy spotting a Greco-Roman reference in literature and find a well-crafted tricolon crescens an absolute delight, but no one looks at a Monet merely to count the brush strokes. How often do we make a reading, especially in English or world language classes, merely a mining expedition for figures of speech, historical facts, or salutary aphorisms? Do we ever with our students simply read a poem, listen to a piece of music, or observe a work of nature or art and then do nothing more?

I can hear the objections rising even in my own mind as the presumed need for assessments and productivity claims the honor of precedence that we have yielded to it. My colleague's student, however, was right. In addition to all the pragmatic facets of education and the demonstrable proofs of their having been mastered, we need as well those facets that "transport us into a space in our minds that is purely creative and imaginative." I hope to remember this as I plan future explorations for my own students into, as Poe in "To Helen" put it "the glories that were Greece and the grandeur that was Rome."[18]

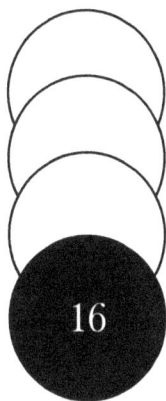

16 Teaching in a Coat and Tie

I have always taught in a coat and tie. Never in my career have I been required to do so, nor am I making a fashion statement. As far as that goes, my sartorial selections are quite traditional, e.g., navy jacket with tan or gray slacks, blue tie with gray jacket and navy slacks, and so forth. My reason for how I dress to teach each day is rooted in one of the most fundamental aspects of my teaching philosophy, the importance of modeling.

I am speaking here of what the historian Livy meant in the preface to his *Ab Urbe Condita*. He begins his 142-book history of Rome from its founding to the death of Drusus in 9 A.D. by stating his desire that his readers pay close attention to *quae vita, qui mores fuerint*, the life and habits of life that once were. Cicero had earlier said something similar in his speech *Pro Archia*, an ostensibly defense oration that was more of an encomium on learning. He asks rhetorically, "*Quam multas nobis imagines – non solum ad intuendum, verum etiam ad imitandum – fortissimorum virorum expressas scriptores et Graeci et Latini reliquerunt?*"[19] "How many images have both Greek and Latin authors left us, not only for gazing at, but also for imitating?"

What do an ancient Roman historian and statesman-cum-philosopher have to do with how I dress to teach high school students? They both speak to the importance of models of behavior. I dress as I do because that is how my dad dressed. He had been an elementary teacher before I was born, but as I grew up, I knew him as an elementary school principal.

A photograph that was converted into a painting and hung in his school when he retired represents the image of my dad that I saw every day when he came home from work. It was a professional look, one that conveyed respect for his job as an educator and the people with whom he worked. When I began teaching at a middle school in Kansas City, he was the model for my own apparel. In fact, it was not until years later that I realized why I had made the dress decisions that I had. At the time it simply seemed the natural thing to do.

Surely, you must be thinking, this cannot be the point of this essay. There must be a more significant purpose to this, and indeed there is. Cicero and Livy were right. Imitation is far more than a form of flattery, sincere or otherwise. It is a foundational principle of learning, and this is part of why Cato the Elder's definition of an orator, quoted by Quintilian in *Institutio Oratoria* 12.1.1, was "*Vir bonus dicendi peritus.*" For both Cato and Quintilian, the ideal orator was not merely a person skilled in speaking, but a good person skilled in speaking. It was not enough to learn phrasing and breath control and all manner of rhetorical devices. These cannot exist in a vacuum but must be used by particular human beings, and what kind of people they are matters as much as the abilities they express. The Stoic philosopher Seneca gave voice to this in his Epistle 88 in which he suggested that rather than spending a great deal of time to earn the title *O hominem litteratum*, O well-read man, "*Simus hoc titulo rusticiore contenti: O virum bonum!*" "Let us," he argues, "be content with a more rustic title: O good man!"

Perhaps this is the reason that imitation of the true, the good, and the beautiful is rarely discussed in schools of education or in professional development conferences. We have always, even in Seneca's time, distanced ourselves from that which smacked of the rustic because of an urban prejudice that values the supposed sophistication of the city over anything else. It is helpful, as with any prejudice, to forego judgment until one has examined all sides fully, and once this is done regarding imitation of the good person, it will become clear why this should be a foundational educational principle and not merely a quaint rustic notion best forgotten.

Simply put, we do not like hypocrites. We are unlikely to take seriously the advice to quit cigarettes if it is given by our chain-smoking doctor. Once again, it is Seneca who speaks to this in Epistle 52 and summarizes the idea by admonishing his readers, "*Eum elige adiutorem quem magis admireris cum videris quam cum audieris.*" "Choose a guide whom you admire more when you see him than when you listen to him."

As a teacher I am called to a certain nobility of character. Since I am a Latin teacher, that character should reflect the nobility and beauty of thought and creation expressed by the best of the ancient Greeks and Romans. Teaching involves incarnation. It is not enough that I dictate facts that students could just as easily and possibly better glean from a text or online source. I must embody what I teach, for it is the witness of my life that will produce the most memorable lesson.[20]

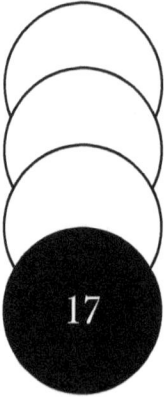

17 Leadership Lessons

What does it say about an organization or business, a school or a church, a team or a group, when its best people start leaving?

My second-year Latin students have been reading selections from Samuel Clarke's 1720 Latin translation of the *Iliad*. They had previously learned some of the rudiments of Greek and had just finished reading parts of Julius Caesar's account of his war in Gaul. By diving into a Latin translation of the Iliad, a war poem originally written in Greek, they were able to bring both of those strands together. Among the many themes and ideas that can be drawn from this roaring adventure story are lessons in leadership. In fact, the entire epic could be read as a case study in leadership styles, but one key thing leapt out recently as we discussed the argument between Agamemnon and Achilles in Book I.

Upon learning that the plague in the Greek camp outside Troy had been caused by Agamemnon's capture of a Trojan girl who was the daughter of a priest of Apollo, Agamemnon was persuaded to return her to her father. He demanded, however, that one of the other Greek soldiers replace his lost war prize with one of their own captured Trojan women. Achilles found this intolerable, arguing that each warrior had won his spoils of war fairly and should not be forced to give up anything. Set aside for a moment the moral issue of taking human slaves as war prizes and notice what happened next. When Agamemnon retaliated against Achilles and his defense of the soldiers' spoils by threatening to taking Achilles's own slave woman, Achilles replied in lines 169-170,

νῦν δ᾽ εἶμι Φθίηνδ᾽, ἐπεὶ ἦ πολὺ φέρτερόν ἐστιν
οἴκαδ᾽ ἴμεν σὺν νηυσὶ κορωνίσιν....

Nunc itaque abeo in Phthiam: quoniam multo melius est,
Domum ire cum navibus rostratis....

Now, therefore, I leave for Phthia, since it is much better
To go home with my beaked ships....

Achilles was far and away the greatest of the Greek warriors in the Trojan War. No warrior worthy of the name would leave the fight, but here was Achilles himself willing to pack up and head for home. It was an issue Agamemnon would have to deal with over the course of the *Iliad*, but it brings up a point that my students and I discussed. When good, qualified people start to leave, leaders need to start asking the hard questions of themselves.

One article in *The Wall Street Journal*,[21] in a seemingly endless series of articles about teachers leaving education, talks about companies that are snatching up educators who are, like Achilles, departing from the fight. Unfortunately, the article makes only one brief reference to "dealing with challenging...administrators" as a cause for the teacher exodus, yet I would argue that it is one of the primary reasons for it.

To have an idea of how the leaders of an organization set the tone for and influence their employees, consider the following email from my current principal to his staff regarding the cancellation of school for inclement weather. After laying out the details and discussing what we needed to do with our students, he concluded, "Last, but not least, enjoy your time at home. God must have thought we needed a break."

You do not need to be a person of any faith at all to recognize the generous humanity in his comment. And what did that inspire in me? It made me want to share that generosity of spirit with my students, and so, when I messaged them about assignments to be completed during our time away from school, I added, "Most importantly, call to mind these words from Roman poet Horace in *Ode* I.9.1-6."

Vides ut alta stet nive candidum
Soracte nec iam sustineant onus
silvae laborantes geluque
flumina constiterint acuto?

Dissolve frigus ligna super foco
large reponens...

Do you see how Mt. Soracte stands gleaming
With deep snow and the struggling forests
Do not sustain their burden and
The rivers are frozen with sharp ice?

Melt the cold as you place upon the hearth
A large stack of wood...

As I work on other school matters during this snow day and drink a cup of Earl Grey, I cannot help but think that if Agamemnon had been more like my principal, Achilles would have stayed. I am quite certain that if more building and district level leaders in education followed his model, we would not be facing such a sharp crisis in education.

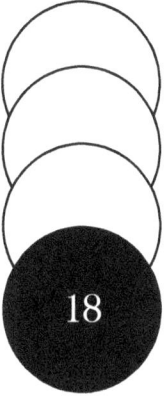

18 Imagining Education

Imagine a square on a piece of paper. Now, imagine stretching that square upward from the surface of the paper. You would have a cube, right? Try, if you can, to imagine expanding that cube into four spatial dimensions. You cannot really do it, because our brains only think in three spatial dimensions (length, width, height), but if you could, you would be imagining a tesseract or a hypercube. About the best that we can visualize in our three-dimensional world is an unfolded hypercube, such as we see in Salvador Dali's 1954 painting *Corpus Hypercubus*.

In an age in which I can pull from my pocket a device that allows me both to see and hear a friend halfway around the world as we converse in real time, we may be losing our sense of amazement at imagination itself. What was, not too many years ago, the province of science fiction is now mundane science. We can certainly imagine amazing things, and we do on a regular basis, both in the design of products and in our entertainment, but then again, it is not that hard to do so. We have split the atom and walked on the moon. We have taken images of far-flung space and helped a 3,000-year-old mummy speak.[22] Should it be surprising that we have imagined the universe of Marvel comics onto the silver screen? To see how amazing human imagination truly is, consider some of what we imagined when we did not have technological marvels on every corner.

In Book IV of his *Metamorphoses*, the Roman poet Ovid told the story of Venus and Mars. It was an adulterous affair between the goddess of love and the god of war, and to get revenge, Vulcan, the husband of Venus and blacksmith of the gods, crafted a net of bronze in which to trap them. Ovid wrote that the strands of the net *lumina fallere possent*. They could deceive the human eye. The net was so finely woven that it would move with the slightest touch and was unlike anything that a weaver or even a spider could spin. Ovid, writing at the beginning of the first century A.D., imagined this adulterer's trap at a time when it could not have been produced in reality. There were many excellent craftsmen of that day, to be sure, but none that could have crafted what Ovid conceived in his mind.

Or take Lucian of Samosata, the second century A.D. satirist who wrote what some consider the first science fiction novel, *True History*, with its wild plot describing travel to the moon and interstellar war. Lucian died sometime around 180 A.D., which is a long time before Neil Armstrong or *Star Wars*. Such a tale from a time when there was no electricity or telescopes is quite imaginative, and knowing the circumstances in which it was written, we likely experience a little wonder, if not jaw-dropping amazement, at the very act of Lucian's imagination.

Imagination is a critical and foundational component of literacy, something I was discussing recently with a former student now preparing at a major university to become an English teacher. As our Zoom conversation wound its way through many ideas, I recalled the story of one of my homeroom students years ago as he took our statewide assessment. One part of the test asked the students to write to a prompt that said something like, "You and your class went on a trip to a dairy farm. Write about what happened on that trip." This young man raised his hand, and when I went to his desk, he quietly said, "I didn't go on that trip." I replied that this was to pretend, that he should imagine what it would have been like and to write about that. He accepted the advice, and as I walked away, I noticed the ankle bracelet that this sophomore was required to wear while on house arrest.

Since he was in my homeroom, which only met once a week, I did not know him well, and I never learned all of his circumstances, but I was shaken deeply that day, and the ripples of that interaction are with me still. I did not know what had warranted his house arrest, but I did know that he lacked a skill necessary for learning, imagination. Whether that had anything to do with his legal trouble, I could not say, but it was heartbreaking to think that a high school sophomore did not recognize an imaginative assignment for what it was or, worse still, lacked the capacity to fulfill it.

Imagination is at the heart of metaphor, and it is possible to see all language as metaphoric. When I look at an object sitting on my desk and tell a friend, "That is my stapler," I have made a comparison, a reference. I have uttered the two-syllable word "stapler," perhaps even written its five consonants and two vowels on a piece of paper, and have asked my friend to connect those sounds and letters with the object on my desk and think of them as the same. It is, when you think about it, an extraordinary act of imagination to think that seven distinct shapes on a piece of paper are the same as a metal and plastic, rectangular device capable of puncturing an object with a slender bit of metal and then bending that metal so that what has been punctured by it cannot readily escape from it. It takes even greater imagination to suppose that an act of exhalation and vocal cord-vibration is equivalent to that metal and plastic, rectangular device. If such imagination is required for the identification of a simple office item, how much do we need to understand math or physics or poetry?

Much goes into the making of imagination, both in terms of the material by which imagination works and the working of that material into what we call imagination. In a similar way, a painting is the product of both physical elements such as paint, brushes, and canvas, along with the training and practice and work of the painter. What, then, are the materials and the working that go into the formation of imagination? The answers, of course, far exceed what can be explored here, but there are some basics that can be considered.

Experience, along with the realization that things can be other than they are, is one of the key elements of imagination. Once I have experienced a coffee cup and have come to understand that its shape may be varied, I can imagine a cup that will ride without spilling in my car, and so the travel mug is born. One of the best ways for me to rapidly expand my experience of the world is through reading. My grandmother used to say that she could go anywhere in a book, and she was right. Faster than in a *Star Trek* transporter, I can be whisked by a book to any place in the universe and at any point in history, and this is one of the reasons why reading is crucial, especially in early childhood. Maryanne Wolf, whose background is in neuroscience and psycholinguistics, has written much about this, and the point is quite simple. Children need to be read to when they are young and need as much experience with reading as they can get once they are able to read for themselves. I will never forget when one of my students asked if I had read Seamus Heaney's then new translation of *Beowulf*. When I said that I had not, he offered to bring it to me when his dad had finished reading it. As excited as I was to see the new *Beowulf*, I was more struck by the comment about his father's reading habits. Reading was clearly a part of this family's life, not only engaged in with and for the children, but by the adults as well, thus modeling the look of literacy for the younger members.

If reading is a source of experience, one of the necessary ingredients for imagination, how is that experience kneaded and worked into imagination itself? In no small part this happens through imaginative play among children. When my son was little, we ran around the backyard in endless re-enactments of the Trojan War. He was always the victorious Achilles, and I the doomed Hector, and there can be no doubt that the imaginative play of his youth, which included adventures with toy knights and kingdoms built of Legos, shaped the imagination that he now uses as an industrial design major. Whether it is retelling a story through a classroom play complete with cardboard props and costumes cobbled together from the rummage sale to drawing pictures of a favorite story in a notebook, this sort of creative and recreative work is essential for developing the skill of imagining.

St. Anselm (1033-1109) is famous for putting forth his ontological proof for the existence of God. In *Proslogion* 2 he says that God is *aliquid quo maius nihil cogitari potest*, that than which no greater can be imagined. He is the very limit of our imagination because He is the source of our imagination, and it certainly takes imagination on our part even to attempt to get our minds around how John described the incarnation of Christ in his gospel when he wrote that the Word was God and the Word became flesh and lived among us. Our word "imagination" is derived from the Latin word *imago*, which we find in Colossians 1:15 where Jesus is described as the *imago Dei*, the image of God. Just a few lines later in verse 19 we read that all the fullness of God dwelled in Him. Once again, Jesus, Who is God, is the very limit of our imagination. He is the fullness of God. He is that which nothing greater can be imagined.

Imagination is necessary not only for attempting to grasp theological concepts, but for the living out of faith as well. Christians understand themselves as living in the world of already-but-not-yet. Christ is already victorious over all things, and yet we await His return and the renewal of all things. This is why His description in Revelation 4:8 as the One Who was, Who is, and Who is to come, while seemingly illogical, makes sense, but it does take a stretching of our imagination to get there. What does it mean, then, to live in such a reality? We are everyday imagining new ways of doing just that.

Much more can be and has been written about imagination, but I want to close by revisiting the idea of reading. Not only do books quickly broaden our experiences, the raw material of our imagination, but they allow us to see how others imagine. For most of human history, people have learned skills through apprenticing, by seeing how others have done something, and this applies well to developing our imagination. When we see how master authors, both of fiction and nonfiction, have imagined the tale they have to tell, we see yet another way for us to imagine our own tale, a way that we can follow or that will inspire us to imagine something new yet again.

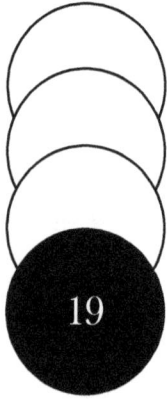

19 Brazen Chains of Madness

In Book I of the *Aeneid*, Jupiter describes to Venus a coming age of peace for the as yet unfounded Roman people. One of the features of that peace was that Madness

> *saeva sedens super arma, et centum vinctus aenis*
> *post tergum nodis, fremet horridus ore cruento.*

> Upon its savage weapons and bound with a hundred bronze knots
> Behind its back will frightfully roar with its bloody mouth. (*Aeneid* I.295-296)

But what if those brazen chains were created by insanity itself? Surely those bound would also roar frightfully, and so they do in the halls of many American schools.

I recently attended a conference during which those in my session shared some of the evaluative practices in their schools. As soon as one teacher mentioned having to provide documentation of various instructional practices for year-end evaluation, the others almost unanimously chimed in to share their own experiences of the sort of top-down hamstringing of educators that is all too common. I immediately thought of the scene in the movie *Gladiator* in which Maximus exclaims to his trainer, "Marcus Aurelius had a dream that was Rome, Proximo. This is not it. This is not it!"

Imagine Pope Julius II requiring Michelangelo to document how he involved the painters on his team in the painting of the Sistine Chapel ceiling. Imagine the great painter being forced to provide evidence for the different approaches to fresco he had employed. Would it not have been better simply to gaze at the finished ceiling in awe and wonder?

This insanity of binding our teachers with chains of bronze stems from treating education like a quantifiable, natural science, which it is not. It stems from the belief that such control improves learning. It stems from the belief that a pseudo-scientific veneer will give credibility to a maligned profession. It stems from the need to justify various administrative positions created to orchestrate this circus of bedlam, a word used here in its original sense as a colloquial pronunciation of "Bethlem," the infamous mental hospital in London.

I do not suffer from such professional indignity, such deliberate obstruction of true education, at the school where I currently teach, but far too many of my friends and colleagues in other schools do, and this is one reason why private, public charter, hybrid, and homeschool models have the freedom to operate more nimbly and efficiently than traditional, public schools do. As I once told a friend who was on the school board of the public school district in which we had taught together, this should bother you, but the response should not be to shackle non-public educators in a similar way, but rather to remove the ridiculous restraints from all teachers.

A good friend of mine who is not in the field of education replied after I had told him about the experience with my conference colleagues mentioned above, "Bureaucrats will, by nature, legislate the life out of innovators and entrepreneurs – leaving organizations highly regulated but without a pulse." Any good teacher at the primary, secondary, or university level can testify to the truth of that statement, and tax-paying citizens should know that this is what is happening in their schools. Would you rather the teacher of your child spend his or her time designing creative ways to help their students learn from the past and prepare for the future or in keeping track of artifacts to prove whether a particular approach to teaching was used the correct percentage of the time?

In 1996 Alan Sokal, physics professor at NYU and University College London, published an article in *Social Text*, a journal of postmodern culture studies. The article was titled "Transgressing the Boundaries: Towards a Transformative Hermeneutics of Quantum Gravity"[23] and proposed that quantum gravity was nothing more than a social and linguistic construct. The article was sheer nonsense, and Sokal's aim was to expose academic publishing for the Emperor's New Clothes that it too often peddled. The article was published, and a few weeks later Sokal revealed the whole thing had been a hoax.

I am willing to bet that most teachers today will recognize the nonsense jargon of Sokal's article title. Consider for a moment the following paragraph.

"If one examines precapitalist deappropriation, one is faced with a choice: either reject constructivist capitalism or conclude that art may be used to marginalize minorities. But Marx uses the term 'precapitalist deappropriation' to denote the paradigm of post-semantic sexual identity. A number of discourses concerning deconstructivist neocultural theory exist."

To the teachers reading this, I ask how similar that sounds to something you were supposed to read for a professional development session you have attended. It is precisely the kind of thing we are used to, and yet that paragraph came from an article that was intentionally created as pure nonsense at elsewhere.org/pomo. The creators of the site use a tool called the Dada Engine, "a system for generating random text from recursive grammars." As they note on their website, "The essay you have just seen is completely meaningless and was randomly generated by the Postmodern Generator."[24]

A fellow graduate student asked me one day years ago if the lunch I was heating up in the office microwave were vermicelli with red sauce. It was rather obviously just spaghetti, yet "vermicelli with red sauce" apparently sounded more sophisticated. Educators everywhere must resist the urge to use jargon and the pseudo-scientific collection of data as if doing so actually improves teaching and learning or gives any respect to our profession. It does not. It is merely laughable. Teaching is a difficult calling. Some cannot understand and respect that, but posturing merely hinders the work of teachers who are leading their students on the shared journey of discovery that is education and working to correct the true causes of failing education.

Parents as well must not be fooled by lofty language and jargon about time spent by their children's teachers on some of the practices of their job. One of my students' parents used to ask me about what teachers were being asked to do in the school where I taught. She was involved in what was going on in the lives of her children, as she should have been. If your "Spidey senses" begin to tingle when you hear what is happening in the lives of your children's teachers, if you begin to sense that "something is rotten in the state of Denmark," then dig a bit deeper. If it turns out that those teachers are being bound by the brazen chains of madness, help them to break free by telling administrators and school board members that you will not accept it. Good schools see their enrollments increase and teaching positions easily filled. Bad schools do not.

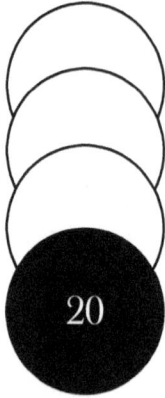

Ancient Outer Space and the Capacity of Students

20

A search for space aliens and antiquity will take you into some of the stranger parts of the Internet, but is the idea of intelligent life on another planet merely a staple of modern science fiction? As it turns out, humans have been giving this some thought for more than 2,500 years.

While preparing for one of the most exciting units of study with a high school class, I ran across a quotation from Lactantius, the early Christian author who was an advisor to the Roman emperor Constantine at the time of his conversion to Christianity. A quick search for the Latin text at Documenta Catholica Omnia,[25] one of the largest text repositories on the Internet, turned up the quotation and a bit more.

Xenophanes...dixit, intra concavum lunae sinum esse aliam terram et ibi aliud genus hominum simili modo vivere quo nos in hac terra vivimus. Fuisse Seneca inter Stoicos ait, qui deliberaret utrumne Soli quoque suos populos daret. Sed, credo, calor deterrebat ne tantam multitudinem periculo committeret. (Institutiones Divinae III.23)

Xenophanes said that there was another earth inside the hollow bosom of the moon and that there another race of humans lived in a similar manner as we live on this earth. Seneca said that among the Stoics was one who deliberated whether he should also attribute to the Sun its own peoples. But, I believe, the heat deterred him lest he commit such a great number of people to danger. (*Divine Institutes*, III.23)

It is amusing how Lactantius dismisses the unnamed Stoic's idea of a population on the Sun by suggesting he did not want even in theory to condemn a race of people to such burning heat, but pause to consider that someone was even thinking about this in the time of Seneca, which was the first century A.D. Even more striking is that Xenophanes, a Greek philosopher who lived from about 570 to about 478 B.C., kicked around a notion of another planet full of human beings existing inside the moon more than two thousand, five hundred years ago. Lactantius scornfully disregarded that idea as well, but what is striking is how imaginative these ancient thinkers were.

One of the things I love about academic life, whether lived out principally in elementary and secondary schools or at the undergraduate and graduate levels, is the discovery that comes from research rabbit trails. While preparing for a new unit in a high school second-year Latin class, I chanced upon a quotation in a footnote that caught my attention. That quotation led me to the original text of a Latin author from the third-to-fourth centuries, which in turn revealed the amazing imagination of a man named Xenophanes, who lived two and a half millennia and half a world away from my own time and place. As I have said countless times in talks and in writing, education is a shared journey of discovery.

Ad astra per aspera. To the stars through difficulties. The path to the stars has indeed been a difficult and a long one, perhaps longer than many realize, stretching back as it does to the age of Classical antiquity. The unit for which I had been preparing when I ran across the passage from Lactantius was one in which my second-year Latin students read selections from Plato, Aristotle, and Cicero about space, along with parts of the first science fiction novel, *True History*, written by Lucian of Samosata in the second century

A.D. These students translated and discussed ancient works on outer space. They worked from Latin renditions of Plato, Aristotle, and Lucian, whose originals were in Greek, and the Cicero from his own Latin. They were introduced to ancient technology through the Antikythera Mechanism, a device dating to the second century B.C. for calculating astronomical positions, and ancient mathematics through the calculation of the earth's circumference by Eratosthenes. They explored the music of the spheres with NASA's discovery of the sound of black holes[26] and the classical music of Gustav Holst and his orchestral suite, *The Planets.*

One part of the unit about which I was particularly excited came at the end. After three weeks of deep study in ancient readings on space, our students met a friend of mine via Zoom. Neil Jenkins and I go back to first grade in our friendship, but I did not bring him in for us to discuss our fondness for '80s music and *Miami Vice.* He holds a Ph.D. from the University of Alabama and has a background in lasers, quantum optics, and theoretical quantum physics. He retired from the federal government in 2023 and serves as the Chief Scientist for the General Dynamics Quantum Engineering Center in Scottsdale, Arizona.

He talked with the students about quantum physics, laser physics, and astrophotography, along with how his Christian faith and work as a scientist fit perfectly together. When students were asking for his email, asking me for copies of his slides, and staying after class to discuss further the wonders of space, I knew this had been a meaningful event.

As soon as the last bell of the day had rung, another small group of students came to the room for a leadership meeting about a Latin club event. My intent was to let them handle everything, and I doubt I could have added much that afternoon anyway. My mind and heart were already too full from the Zoom class with Dr. Jenkins. As it turned out, I was not needed. These student officers led with such efficiency they could have given a lesson to many adults. They worked together, listened to each other's ideas, and yet did not become stuck in the mire of indecision. Just when I thought my heart could take no more of being impressed with students, I was overwhelmed by their display of leadership skills. In Book I of the *Aeneid,* Vergil describes Queen Dido by saying, *dux femina facti,* the leader of the deed was a woman.

In this case, the leaders of the deed were students, and I could have offered nothing that would have made their work better. On the drive home, I called my wife and more or less babbled. I could not find the words to describe these extraordinary young people and was reminded of a scene in *Contact*, the 1997 movie featuring Jodie Foster as Dr. Ellie Arroway, who takes a trip through a wormhole to another part of the universe. Stupefied at what she sees, all she can say is that instead of a scientist, they should have sent a poet.

For many people, the phrase "life's rich pageant" is familiar because it is the title of the fourth album by alternative rock band R.E.M., although it has a much longer history. I reach for that phrase often, for it captures perfectly what is my typical experience of academic and educational life. Have I known the sorts of stories that are driving so many people out of the education profession? I have, but they have never been the norm. When given the opportunity, young people will be astonished with the depth of their thought and their ability to do something with it, and I saw it once again that day.

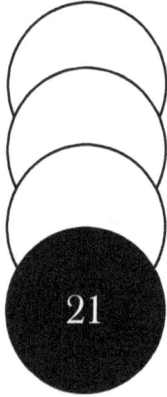

Swimming in the Deep End

The deep end of the pool has many advantages. You can usually dive in without breaking your neck. You can float more easily. You can do twists and turns and readily let your imagination take you into the realms of Atlantis or whatever fantasy you wish to play out.

It is the end of the semester for my Advanced Placement Latin students, and while I am sure the activity we have pursued for the past three days has been useful in preparing for their final exam, it has, more importantly, given them a chance to swim in the deep end. We have been exploring various translations of Vergil's epic poem, the *Aeneid*. They range from the 17th century version of Dryden to the 2009 rendering by Sarah Ruden, the first complete translation made by a woman. Some of the translations are prose, and others are poetry.

On the first day of this exercise, the class picked a passage they had read from Book I, another from Book II, and a third from Book IV. They chose translations from one of our shelves, or in the case of one young lady, on her computer, and their task was to analyze each of the three passages for grammatical changes, such as whether an originally plural word had become singular in translation. They then shared their findings, and we discussed why a translator may have made certain changes.

The second day saw them doing the same thing, but with the focus on content. Had the translator added, subtracted, or changed anything of significance apart from the grammar? This led to a discussion of what changes were legitimate and what effect they had on understanding the *Aeneid*.

Today was our final round of this work. The students worked in small groups, and each group chose its own passage, one we had read in Latin but that had not been discussed the other two days. The students then read the published translations of their passages and shared the translations with each other so that each member of each group could read all the translations within the group. Their task this time was more personal. They simply had to pick the translation they liked best.

As their time of reading and reflection drew to a close, I put three questions on the board. "Why do you prefer one translation and not another?" "What criteria are you using to choose?" "What are you looking for?"

I did not give these questions until the end because I wanted the students to be free to engage with the texts however they chose and then to reflect on the process. Not surprisingly, their answers were intriguing.

We began with the last question, and most said they were looking for a translation that was readable and understandable, one without archaic English. As Matthias put it in his own, inimitable way, "I want a median between the vulgate and what is dripping with exaggeration." Another student said, "Yeah, what he said, only in normal language." When we moved to discussing how they made their choice of favorite once they had read several different translations, the emphasis still seemed to be on readability, but Ayrrana said something different. She said that she focused on word choice and whether or not a translator used a word that was too big or too small for the passage. If the translator used "run" where "dashed" would have seemed better to her, she rejected the translation as being too small.

I will keep a secret the translations the students preferred and those they did not, although I will say that one made it on both lists! What was important was how these young scholars grappled with the subtleties and art of professional translations. They had a sufficient grasp of the original to be able to offer meaningful critiques, and this exploration opened them up to a wider range of work and also allowed them to put themselves into it.

Into That Good Night

22

Nature, and Nature's Laws lay hid in Night.
God said, "Let Newton be!" and All was Light.[27]
Alexander Pope

It may seem odd that an essay by someone from the field of Classical Studies in a book about education is principally about a physics movie. Those who make it through to the end of it, and who know me, will perhaps not think it so strange.

This essay is an attempt for me to grasp the physics-poem that is the film *Interstellar*, starring Matthew McConaughey and Anne Hathaway, which was released in 2014. For 169 minutes when I first saw it at the theater, I sat with my eyes wide open, riveted to the unfolding of the mysteries of reality in cinematic metaphor as multiple dimensions, quantum physics, and the beautiful strangeness of space-time were breathtakingly imagined on screen.

When I was a graduate student in Classics at The University of Texas, my wife and I went one evening to a local mall, and as was my habit, I headed to the bookstore. I ended up with CUNY physics professor Michio Kaku's book *Hyperspace* in my hands, and my life very nearly took a significant turn. I read a good portion of the book while standing in the bookstore, and when my wife insisted we must leave, I purchased the book and began babbling all the way home about quantum physics and a possible change of graduate work. Kaku's book led me to everything from Dali's *Corpus Hypercubus* to Edwin Abbott's *Flatland*[28] to a Caltech physicist named Kip Thorne, who had published an article about the possibility of time travel. This sent me running to the physics, math, and astronomy library at U.T. to find the article,[29] and suddenly I could think of nothing else but superstrings and multiple dimensions.

How does a person describe what it is like to catch a glimpse into the possible physical structure of reality? As I lacked a sufficient physics and mathematics background to do so, one of my few true and deep regrets in life, I ended up staying with Classics, a choice I have never regretted. Still, as Pope famously cautioned, one must be careful of drinking from the Pierian spring. Once I had sipped this particular elixir of the Muses, I returned numerous times for longer draughts, always savoring certain aspects of physics through metaphor if not through mathematics.

Then came *Interstellar*. It was everything I experienced in that Texas bookstore, but brought to life, or as close to life as a three-dimensional representation of the fourth dimension of time can be on a two-dimensional screen. And as the credits rolled, there was the name of the executive producer Kip Thorne.

So why am I really writing about this? The film makes repeated use of Dylan Thomas's famous villanelle, "Do Not Go Gentle Into That Good Night" and for a variety of reasons beyond the scope of this essay. Yet one reason must surely be to push against the dark boundaries of ignorance. There is so much that we have yet to learn about everything. That is what drives me, the unbridled desire and passion to learn. The darkness in which lies hidden all that we do not know is not a bad darkness. It is a good night, for it undoubtedly contains much truth, goodness, and beauty, and it is into that good night I am eager to lead my students on our shared journey of discovery.

To Be a Child?

23

And in my heart you will remain forever young. – Rod Stewart

When I was a child, I spoke like a child, I thought like a child, I reasoned like a child. When I became a man, I gave up childish ways. – 1 Corinthians 13:11, ESV

At a school where I once taught, we offered a scholarship each year to one of our graduating seniors from our Latin program. Part of the application required that candidates pick a Latin quotation and use it as the basis for a discussion of the benefit of Classics to them and of their own interest in Classics. One year an applicant chose, "*Nescire autem quid ante quam natus sis acciderit, id est semper esse puerum.*" This is Cicero's famous statement, "Not to know what happened before you were born is to remain forever a child," and it comes from his work *Orator*, 119. At the end of a thoughtful essay, that student, who had begun Latin study as an 8th grader and thus took five years and prepared for the Advanced Placement and International Baccalaureate tests along the way, had this to say.

"Being able to understand and parse themes from the Classical era develops a mindset for understanding the out-of-reach parts of the world, separated by either time or by distance. That ability turns a person from a child, trapped in a singular world of self, to a person of the world, conscientious of those they have never met and may never meet.

"So ask me why I have spent the last five years studying a dead language of a people long since passed. Ask me why I have bothered to translate Classical works from Latin instead of just reading someone else's translation. Ask me why it matters if Horace was able to openly attack his contemporaries in his satires like his predecessor Lucilius or not. My answer will remain the same: I refuse to remain a child when I can be a person of the world."

It is not news to say that ours is a youth-obsessed age. The old advertising jingle "I don't want to grow up. I'm a Toys R Us kid," is the theme song of the present day. I do not know whether this is the cause or the consequence of our failure to expose children to the great works of literature, art, and music. Likely as not the two are now caught in a vicious cycle. Anthony Esolen, in an article for the journal *Public Discourse*, sounds the alarm by merely stating the facts. Would that those who had ears to hear should do so. In that article, he cites Henry Van Dyke from an 1893 piece in which Van Dyke will not give in to pessimism with regard to literature, but expects a recovery from poets who merely "please a degenerate race with the short-lived melodies of earthly delight and the wild chants of withering passion."[30] Esolen, however, is quite certain that Van Dyke was wrong.

I would tend to agree with Esolen with regard to our literary and cultural landscape. Yet there are, as there have always been, the remnants who know and are shaped by the true, the good, and the beautiful. They are as Aeneas described the Trojan refugees in *Aeneid* I.30, "*reliqui[ae] Danaum et immitis Achilli*," the offscourings, if not of the Danaans and savage Achilles, of a society whose systems of education no longer read to become human and to make connection with humanity, but for much duller, more ephemeral, and sadly utilitarian ends.

I say these remnants exist, for I am blessed to see them in my classes. Will those who read Caesar and Cicero, Horace and Vergil in high school turn the monstrous and sinking ship of our society, barnacled as it is with grotesqueries imaginable in another age perhaps only to a Dante? *Titanic*'s rudder was indeed too small. Yet small is also the mustard seed, and while I am not sure I have its quantity of faith, I do have at least that amount of hope, and that hope stems from students like this senior.

24

The Disposition to Learn

Being willing to be told one is wrong is a necessary disposition for learning.

Docility is crucial for a learner. In fact, it is a necessary condition for learning, which means that without it, learning cannot occur. Unfortunately, docility, or the quality of being docile, has taken on the sense of being quiet and meek, shy and retiring, unable or unwilling to raise one's voice. Yet, as with so many ideas and words in English, if we look at the Latin root we come to a better understanding. The word "docility" comes from that Latin verb *docere*, meaning "to teach." Docility is, therefore, quite simply the quality of being able to be taught, which is not an inherent quality or one shared by all people at all times. In other words, not everyone is docile. Not everyone can be taught.

Consider for a moment the obvious. You could not be taught how to change the oil in your car if you were asleep. Your dormant state would leave you incapable of learning. The same would be true if you were listening to music loud enough to render people unconscious.[31] Unable to hear what the instructor was saying, you could not learn. You would likely learn little to nothing about changing your car's oil if you were being instructed while observing the bone protruding from your broken leg. The intense pain and shock would make you less than docile.

These, of course, are circumstantial limitations to docility, and many people recognize similar limitations at work in the lives of school-aged children. Poverty, violence, and abuse are but three.

Yet there are other behaviors, attitudes, and mindsets that can limit or entirely block, or foster or support a student's docility. Some of these are derivative of circumstances and others are within the direct control of students themselves, but taken together they form the disposition for learning that every student brings into the classroom, and it is this disposition that determines whether a student at any given moment in any given subject is docile enough to learn.

Perhaps the most significant attitude leading to a docile disposition is the willingness to be told that one is wrong. Consider two proverbs and the lyrics to a pop song.

Whoever loves discipline loves knowledge, but he who hates reproof is stupid. (Proverbs 12:1, ESV)

Whoever ignores instruction despises himself, but he who listens to reproof gains intelligence. (Proverbs 15:32, ESV)

One night, me with my big mouth,
Couple guys had to put me in my place.
When I see those guys these days,
We just laugh and say,
"Do you remember when?" ("Cherry Bomb," John Mellencamp)

It is no insult to be told that you are wrong about something. Admittedly, there are better and worse ways of telling someone this, but regardless of how the information is communicated, we must be willing to accept it when it is true or we cannot learn. It is a necessary, a without-which-not characteristic of being docile.

One of the best ways parents and those entrusted with the care and nurture and education of young children can prepare them for a lifetime of learning is to help them understand what it means when they are told that they are wrong about something. It means that they are wrong, nothing more and nothing less. It does not mean that they are bad. It is not a statement about their character, unless, of course, that about which they are wrong is a moral action. It does not mean that the one stating the fact thinks ill of them or will no longer love them. This last statement is vital to understanding this key component of docility. My telling a student that he or she has formed a verb incorrectly in no way indicates my lack of love for that student, but rather is proof of my care and concern. I would not want my students to make fools of themselves by writing something incorrectly. I love them too much.

To be sure, this is a mature concept to grasp, but then education is largely an enterprise for the mature of any given age. Those called to the shared journey of discovery that is education must help those on the way know how to accept when they have been told that they are headed down a wrong path.

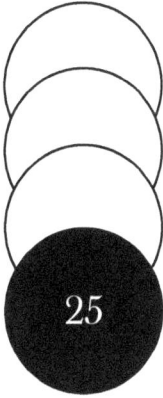

Don't Show Me Your Plans

25

There is an old joke that if you want to make God laugh, tell Him your plans. If you want to give teachers one more reason to quit, ask to see theirs.

I have heard many stories from my mother about her elementary teaching career in the late 1950s and throughout the 1960s. They often involved her beloved principal, Mr. Montgomery. Among her favorites is the one in which he told her, a young teacher early on the shared journey of discovery that is education, why he did not need to see her lesson plans each week as other principals did. He considered her a professional and trusted her to do her job.

She reflected many times how good that made her feel. She was new to the profession, but this seasoned educational leader trusted her, and he proved it by not looking over her shoulder or micromanaging what she did in her classroom.

Bad administrators are killing education, and this type of "quality control" is one more weapon in their arsenal. As one *Forbes* article puts it, "No job worth doing breaks down into tiny, measurable parts. Good jobs are whole. You know what your mission is and you work toward your mission every day, checking in with your manager as appropriate. Run away from any company that surrounds you with yardsticks and measurements."[32] Evaluations based on whether or not objectives are displayed in the room or on the proper filling out of suffocating lesson plans and unit planners reveal absolutely nothing about whether teachers are teaching well. They reveal merely a person's ability to snap to attention when the jackboots come marching, their ability to jump through hoops that any sane person would recognize are insulting and ridiculous.

Is there a place for planning in a teacher's life? There most certainly is. When I dream of some fantastic new project for my students, I have to come down out of the clouds and begin to plan. I have to consider what I want them to achieve in the project, what their role and my role should be, what resources we will need, where we will get them if we do not have them, how long we can spend on the project, what must be shifted or removed to make room for it, and a host of other pedagogically responsible factors.

Will anyone see these plans? They may. One of my former colleagues who taught French used to collaborate with me on a project her students and my Latin students would engage in together. We shared these ideas and plans with our department chair, sometimes to get her input, other times to ask for her assistance, and often just to bring her into the sheer fun and excitement of it.

There are also sound reasons for a leader or administrator to see the written plans of a teacher. Pre-service teachers in field experiences or student-teaching programs benefit from the slow, careful process of writing out plans and can gain much from discussing those plans with a trusted leader or mentor. And, of course, there are times when even experienced teachers may need guidance, whether because they are teaching something new or for whatever reason are not at their best. Working with a valued leader on planning can help teachers reach their potential.

But consider what is gained by not requiring veteran teachers who are experts both in their fields and in pedagogy to submit lesson and unit plans for evaluation. It sends the clear message that they are trusted professionals and valued colleagues. Any administrator who has to check whether an objective is written on a board or whether plans have been uploaded in a certain format in order to determine whether a teacher is teaching well should be fired, for that administrator lacks true discernment. Good education leaders are in classrooms. They work with, not above teachers. They watch and listen to students. Do your neighbors really have to knock on your door to tell you they are pulling the lawn mower out of the garage for you to know whether they are maintaining their yards?

My wife and I once needed to clean the blades on our ceiling fans, and our daughter, then age 12, wanted to help. I set up the ladder and showed her how to detach the blades and the glass covering of the light. I helped her a bit on the first fan, but when we took the ladder into another room, I only stood nearby and did not help. At one point she was uncertain if she could hold the glass covering with one hand and unscrew the nut with her other. I told her that although she may have felt uncertain of her abilities, I was quite confident in them and then proved my confidence by not interfering. Can you imagine what it would do for teachers if their administrators demonstrated such confidence in them? My mother did not only imagine it. She remembered it fondly more than fifty years later.

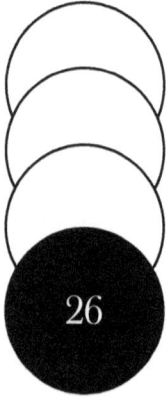

26   A Teacher's Office

In an online group for Latin teachers, one person posted a picture of a bookcase filled with volumes by Greek and Latin authors and wrote, "Whatever else you do this year, remember our OFFICIUM: Keep the voices in these books alive in your students – lest they fall into oblivion. We are so blessed to be Latin teachers!" He went on to say that he had posted his picture and comment because it is easy for teachers to forget why they do what they do. He concluded, "If we fail in our task, who will read Vergil, Tacitus, Caesar, or Cicero in the next generation?"

The word this teacher used, *officium*, is the root of the English word "office," which people far too often think of merely as a place to do work. Yet the Latin suggests much, much more. At its root are the words *opus* and *facere*, meaning "work" and "to do/make." The word opifex meant a craftsman or artificer, and *opificium* described, according to the Oxford Latin Dictionary, "the performance of constructive work." *Officium* was a contraction of opificium and came to have a wide range of meanings including an act of service or respect and one's duty or obligation to another.

Now consider the office of a teacher. We have a duty, indeed even a sacred trust, to pass on what we have learned, and my friend's question has haunted me for several years. In no sequence of high school classes can students plumb the depth or explore the breadth of Classical writing. It is humanly impossible. We do as much as we can, of course, and if we are not going to read Aristotle or Plautus, I can at least mention their names and hope that someday, maybe, one of my students may see those names scrawled in an old notebook and seek out their works.

A quotation from Benjamin Jowett, taken from the preface to his translation of Thucydides, once hung outside my classroom door. "[T]he voluminous learning of past ages [has] to be recast in easier and more manageable forms. And if Greek literature is not to pass away, it seems to be necessary that in every age someone who has drunk deeply from the original fountain should renew the love of it in the world, and once more present that old life, with its great ideas and great actions, its creations in politics and in art, like the distant remembrance of youth, before the delighted eyes of mankind."[33]

Teachers are translators, and this is true whether we teach math or physical education or robotics or Chinese. We carry the ideas of humanity from one age to the next. We have been called to a wonderful, delightful *opificium*, and it is the performance of this most constructive work that is the teacher's true office.

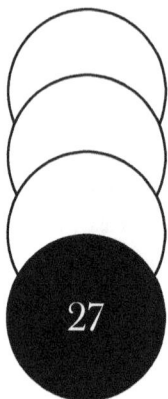

Vague, Sham, Redundant

When my sixth-grade teacher Irvin Goldstein passed from this life to the next, social media was filled with fond remembrances from former students. He was one of the most influential teachers in my education, so it is natural to consider what words come to mind when thinking of him. Several do, actually, and in this order.

Vague

Sham

Redundant

Verbose

Articulate

Gregarious

Mediocre

Magnificent

Loquacious

Although "articulate" and "magnificent" may have described him, the others do not, so you may ask why they come to my mind. Each week Mr. Goldstein put a new word on the chalkboard in addition to our regular spelling list. For extra credit, we could list each word and its predecessors on that week's test. The first week the word was "vague," the second week "sham," and so forth, and I have remembered the first nine in order for more than forty years.

It is not so much that I have a prodigious memory as much as that nearly everything Mr. Goldstein did with his students was memorable. He read to us each day after lunch, and I still recall the excitement of listening to stories such as *Black and Blue Magic* and *Mrs. Coverlet's Magicians*. *Escape From Warsaw* was a book that whisked me away to another place and stayed with me so keenly that I checked it out of our local library and read it to my son when he was young.

And then there were the pickles. Yes, we made pickles. And root beer. In Mr. Goldstein's room, science took on a practical flair, which made sense, given his passion for helping his students engage with the world around them. He took the entire class to his farm for a field trip and designed a camping program for fifth- and sixth-graders that lasted for years in our district. I remember lying out under the stars one evening at Otter Creek Camp, and Mr. Goldstein walked by. He saw my friend Phil and me gazing at the stars and said with a gentle laugh, "They almost seem to move, don't they?"

The two things from his class that had the most significant effect on my education and general life, however, were his instruction in creative writing and his preparation for later stages of learning. He regularly gave us writing prompts, and that was where I came alive. I could not wait for the next writing assignment and began to fill notebooks outside class with my own stories. It was in Mr. Goldstein's room that the writer in me was born.

As for sending us on to junior high and high school, no one could have prepared us better. He treated us as young adults and held us to the highest standards. He equipped us to take notes and organize our time and materials so that the transition to seventh grade and beyond was a smooth one.

My memories of Mr. Goldstein are vivid and far from **vague**, for when it came to teaching, he was no **sham**, but the real deal. I could go on and on, but at some point, my stories would become **redundant** and my writing **verbose** instead of concise as Mr. Goldstein taught. I hope that this meager eulogy has been **articulate** enough, however, to give some insight into a teacher who, while not particularly **gregarious**, was beloved by all, for never would he accept the **mediocre** or anything less than the best from his students. He made us great, and in so doing was the living definition of **magnificent**. Since experiencing sixth-grade with Mr. Goldstein would make even the most taciturn **loquacious** in recalling precious memories, I will end with a simple shalom to one who will always be one of my best teachers.

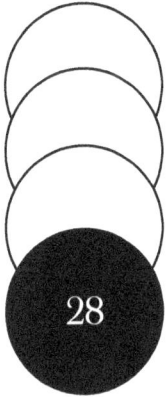

28 Mr. Holland's *Aeneid*

The 1995 film *Mr. Holland's Opus* tells the story of Glenn Holland, an aspiring musician and composer whose dream is to create one memorable work of music. To pay his bills, however, he takes a job as a high school band teacher, never considering that to be his true vocation and spending his evenings laboring over his composition. As Emilio Estevez says to his father, Martin Sheen, in *The Way*, you don't choose a life, you live one, and the one that Mr. Holland lives seems far from the one he would have chosen. As the film develops, both he and the audience discover that his true composition, the opus for which he will be known, is the work he has accomplished with his students.

For many years I have wanted to publish a translation of Vergil's *Aeneid*. I have played with a half dozen or more metrical schemes in which to do it and have considered prose as well. Since 1533 and the Scots translation by Gavin Douglas, there has been a nearly unbroken succession of English renderings up to and including the 21st century. However the concept of need is defined, there can hardly be one for yet another English *Aeneid*. Why, then, have I been lured by the Siren's call of this notoriously difficult task for so many years?

When I was a boy, I played dentist when I came home from the dentist's office, barber after having my hair cut, and teacher following a day of kindergarten. The latter was enacted with my grandmother as my student and largely for the gleeful pleasure of putting a big, red F on her papers, regardless of her actual achievement. The mimetic impulse is in all of us. As children we role play and act out the lives of those around us in preparation for our adult callings, but even adults still feel the pull of mimesis as we wear jerseys bearing the names of a favorite athlete, display posters of a beloved band or album in the garage, or even try keeping up with the Joneses as we rush to purchase the latest technology.

For me, I want to go ever deeper into the amazing, beautiful, moving, haunting, inspiring, magnificent work that Vergil crafted two millennia ago. So taken am I with it that at times I can only nod in mute agreement with Tennyson's eulogy for the nineteenth centenary of the Roman poet's death.

> *I salute thee, Mantovano,*
> *I that loved thee since my day began,*
> *Wielder of the stateliest measure*
> *Ever moulded by the lips of man.*[34]

What that says, in practical terms, is that I have always wanted to translate this poem. I want to get as deep into its words and artistry and story as I possibly can, and this means giving my own performance of it in translation. This desire is not to satisfy any glaring need in the literary world, for there are many, perfectly good translations, although none can, given the nature and limitations of language, completely capture all of Vergil, and that is one of the reasons why I think I have decided to abandon the project. Every translation into any language of a work like this can only result in one seeing through a glass darkly, and in the particular case of the *Aeneid*, many of the translations are deeply tinted windows indeed. The best one can hope for is to produce a lens with the faintest color possible through which to glimpse the original, but try as one may, there will always be that hint of hue to lend a perspective not present in the model.

There is another reason why I suspect I shall never complete a written translation, and it takes us back to the film *Mr. Holland's Opus*. I have, in fact, translated the *Aeneid* countless times as a work of performance art in my high school advanced Latin classes. There, my students and I have explored shades and nuances and subtleties. We have played with synonyms in an attempt to capture the right essence of a word. We have compared and contrasted bits of plot with storylines in other works and have explored artistic expressions in Vergil's poetry alongside not only other works of literature but other genres of art, including music, film, and painting. Whenever I read it with students, I read it anew and discover some wonderful gem that had escaped notice. Seen this way, my translation of the *Aeneid* is not entirely my own, but is a crowdsourced work of living art, not to be read in the paper-and-board books that line a shelf, but to be expressed in the lives of Vergil's audience, those *auditores* who still hear his stately measures echoing across the millennia.

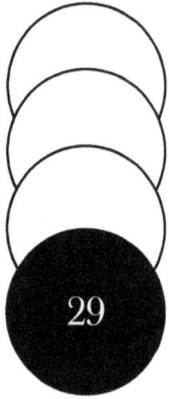

29 Hidden Treasure

As I was scrolling through some old pictures, I ran across one from the title page to a translation of the works of Vergil. Since the picture was in my photos, I realized that I must own the book and immediately remembered not only that I did own it, but where it was on my bookshelves. I ran to that particular bookcase, pulled off the volume, and began to explore what I had.

The oldest translation of Vergil's *Aeneid* in my possession is the 1685 translation by John Dryden, but it is a 20th century edition. Prior to my recent discovery, I had thought the oldest volume in our personal library was the 1794 edition of Cicero's *De Oratore* that I had purchased at an antiquarian bookshop in Florence, Italy. This forgotten edition of Vergil published in 1770 bested that by twenty-four years.

It is the dream of book lovers to discover a long-lost work. Indeed, this idea forms the core of one of the best-selling books of all time, Umberto Eco's *The Name of The Rose*, but let us be clear. I did not unearth on a bookshelf in my Indiana home the lost second book of Aristotle's *Poetics*. Still, just as children enjoy dressing up and playing as their favorite literary or movie characters, I enjoyed the thrill of discovery when I realized just how old this volume was and what it contained.

The book contains the prose translation of Vergil's works. It is, in fact, the first of two volumes (someday, perhaps, I will procure the second), that cover all of the Roman poet's works, the *Eclogues*, the *Georgics*, and the *Aeneid*. The prose rendering is that of Joseph Davidson, originally published in 1743, but this book contains more than a simple translation.

Each page contains the Latin text, a section titled *Ordo* that puts the Latin into more traditionally English word order, Davidson's prose translation, and then copious notes. After the double discovery of the oldest book in my library and a translation of Vergil I did not remember I had, a third thrill of excitement came when I noticed that in Davidson's comparison of the opening lines of the *Aeneid* with those of Homer's *Odyssey*, he cited Alexander Pope's translation after giving the Greek. I have a good friend who is *Beowulf* fan, and he and I love to tease each other about who was the better poet, the *Beowulf* bard or Alexander Pope. For my money, Pope will always win. I have loved his heroic couplets since I was a senior in high school, and his translation of Homer, particularly the *Iliad*, is one of my favorite works of all time. These discoveries alone would have been enough to excite a bibliophile, but something even better was hiding in these three-hundred-year-old pages.

At the beginning of his book, Davidson includes an essay "To Those Gentlemen Who have the immediate Care of Education," and in it he lays out an understanding of education that has been held in various degrees by most people in most cultures, is espoused and practiced by some of us today, but has for too many others become a lost treasure.

Davidson refers to those of us who are teachers as "faithful guides, who, no doubt, will, in whatever author you teach, guard your pupils against the influence of any thing that has a tendency to corrupt their principles or morals" and then goes on to show why Vergil is such a suitable author for this purpose. According to Davidson, "There is a peculiar tenderness and humanity diffused through all his writings, which never fails to make the heart better, and sends away every well disposed mind from the reading of him, equally pleased and improved. He animates the soul to the love of virtue, by setting before us the most noble examples; corrects the passions, by showing their fatal effects, when indulged to excess, or when directed to improper objects; makes us feel the peace and serenity they bring, when conducted by reason, and regulated within the bounds of prudence and moderation. From him we learn the force of piety, and what powerful incentives to fortitude, and every heroic virtue, arise from the belief of a deity, and a providence supremely wise and good. In a word, every image, every description, every character he exhibits; his fables, his allegories, his episodes, all are calculated, not only to please the fancy, but to instruct the judgment, and form the heart."

If that sounds quaint, outdated, or even inappropriate for the modern classroom, it is but sad proof of how far we have drifted from the true purpose of education, which is about far more than teaching mere facts, the sufficient memorization of which can be determined by an exam, and Davidson states this pointedly. "To teach boys to understand an author's language, is, you know, but the least part of your duty. To acquaint them with his spirit and virtuous design, to form their taste aright, that they may be able to correct his faults and relish his beauties, feel the force of his pious or humane sentiments, and learn to copy out his heroic characters, and imitate his generous examples; in a word, to teach them to be sound critics on life and manners and to distinguish the true from the false, ... this is your honourable province, and the chief design of education."

Is that asking too much of our teachers? It is if we insist on placing foolish burdens on them under the guise of professionalism. Earlier in his essay Davidson had explained why he had produced this particular edition of Vergil's works. "If it gives you some relief from the more disagreeable and burdensome part of your work, it is only to leave you freer and more disengaged in the execution of what is the principal business of education." Davidson knew, as have most people in most societies through the ages, that education is a grander enterprise than the mechanical drudgery into which it can be corrupted. He went on to say, "You, by your very profession, are solemnly engaged to teach and exemplify goodness to mankind, at a time of life when they are most capable of being taught, when their docile minds may easily be moulded to every shape of goodness, and are susceptible of the most durable impressions. [T]he legislature may enact, and the magistrate may execute salutary law; but what will all avail, unless the foundations of national virtue be laid in the right forming of the heart at first? If the fountains be foul and impure, all the art of man will not make the streams run pure and unpolluted. The Scripture tells us that the tree must first be made good, and then its fruits will be good also; but if the tree be corrupt, the fruit likewise will partake of the corruption. Indeed experience shows us, that the best education is not of itself sufficient to establish the mind in an habitual, uniform course of integrity; yet the same experience evinces, that nothing is of so much importance towards effecting this great end, as to give the mind an early turn and bias to the right side; and that, without this, all other means, humanly speaking, will have but a weak and transient influence."

The legislature may enact, and the magistrate may execute salutary law; but what will all avail, unless the foundations of national virtue be laid in the right forming of the heart at first? What, indeed.

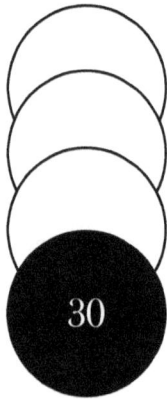

The Tragedy of High School Drama

30

Shakespeare died more than four hundred years ago, and many ask whether there is a place for his work, especially his tragic dramas, either in the drama curriculum of a contemporary high school student or in the entertainment options of the contemporary theater-goer? The answer is yes, and I was recently reminded of why in the most powerful way.

Fear and pity may be aroused by spectacular means; but they may also result from the inner structure of the piece, which is the better way, and indicates a superior poet. For the plot ought to be so constructed that, even without the aid of the eye, he who hears the tale told will thrill with horror and melt to pity at what takes place. But to produce this effect by the mere spectacle is a less artistic method, and dependent on extraneous aids. (Aristotle, *Poetics*, 1453b)[35]

When it comes to non-musical theater, Aristotle suggests that the more powerful play will depend on the words and not the aids of fantastic sets, costumes, or special effects, and that is what I saw in a recent high school production of *Macbeth*.

The set was spare, and the costumes, while perfectly made and fitting, were not so extravagant as to distract. Set changes amounted to nothing more than the occasional moving of a platform on which actors stood, a table, and a few chairs. There was a bit of fog and some simple lighting effects that again enhanced but did not distract from what was of most importance, the words.

The actors' diction and enunciation were clear and powerful, and the choreography of the fight scenes and the scenes with the witches was striking in a way not often found in a high school performance. The audience was drawn deeply into the action, and at many points it was possible to lose sight of the fact that one was watching a play.

Too often adults think that for education to be engaging for students it must connect immediately with their current lives. True education, however, leads us beyond ourselves, past our present boundaries, and into that which transcends our circumstances so that we can become better, and a tragedy such as *Macbeth* does that. The story is larger than that of most of our lives, and because of that we can explore huge themes that we would not ordinarily see. Or to put it another way, we can engage with ideas of power, desire, betrayal, greed, honor, right and wrong, spiritual warfare, and more in the safety of the laboratory that is the theater. To look at just one of those, it is difficult to think meaningfully about betrayal while being betrayed, but in the two hours of a play in which betrayal is being dramatically depicted, we can consider what it means to betray and be betrayed and, hopefully, grow from the experience.

And if you doubt for one moment that teenagers are capable of memorizing long passages marked by unfamiliar words and archaic syntax, let me assure you that they can, and when they have been taught and directed well, they can bring those passages to life in a way that dissolves the strangeness, allowing the audience to enter another story and another world.

Watching a play is entertaining, and so is going to a concert or a movie, and that is just fine. We need entertainment. We need to disengage from the pressures of life for a while and merely let ourselves be entertained. There can be another feature to theater, however, and this is edification. Edification has to do with the building up of a person. It is soul work. It seeks to help others achieve not merely their own dreams, but to become more than they have ever dreamed possible. As Aristotle wrote, this is not achieved best in drama through spectacle, but through the power of words, and there is a reason Shakespeare's works are still being performed more than four centuries after his death. His words are among the best in English at meeting the standard set by Aristotle. His plays, while they can indeed be entertaining, also require something from the audience. They require close listening, a bringing to bear on the story all of our own experiences and knowledge, and a willingness to grow, even through things we may not fully understand.

Tragedy and serious drama have their place in the high school curriculum and in the lives of modern theater-goers. What is truly tragic is when we sell ourselves short by settling for something less.

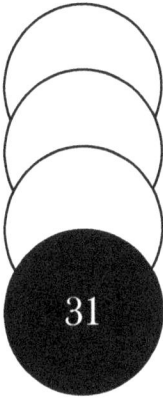

The Way of an Educator

31

They named a road for my dad. This is not the kind of thing to happen every day or for every person, so our family was rather excited about it. The road, Norman R. Perkins Way, is in Floyd County in southern Indiana. It could, of course, have been Norman R. Perkins Street, Avenue, or Road. I am glad they chose "Way," however, for it made me think. Just what was my dad's way, his particular way of doing things?

He was born in 1930 and grew up in Jeffersonville, Indiana, which is on the Ohio River in Clark County. After serving in the Army in Korea, he used the G.I. Bill to earn his undergraduate degree in education from Indiana University. From there he went to the University of Michigan for his Master's in education. After teaching sixth grade there, he moved back home and spent the remaining thirty-three years of his career in the New Albany-Floyd County Consolidated School Corporation. Nine of those years were as a sixth-grade teacher at Mt. Tabor Elementary, and twenty-four were as the principal of Galena Elementary.

When he passed away in 2009, I listened to stories from an unending stream of people at the funeral home. The details may have differed, but they all told the same basic tale, one I had heard from countless colleagues and students of his over the years. Without a doubt, his work as an educator influenced many people, including me. Here are some of his ways.

Dress professionally

My dad did wear Bermuda shorts to mow the grass, but for the five working days of the week and on Sundays for church, my dad wore a coat and tie. When I began my teaching career, I simply never gave any thought to dressing in any other way, and I have done so ever since. We often speak of efforts to professionalize what we do as teachers, and while it is certainly possible to teach Shakespeare in flip flops, I would argue that professionalism has a look. It need not involve a coat and tie *per se*, but when teachers present themselves as if they care about what they do and the trappings in which they do it, they send a clear signal to students that learning is indeed an important endeavor.

Have fun with students

My dad drew smiley faces with ketchup on the hamburgers of his elementary students at lunch time. He added syllables to their names to make them long and funny, eliciting laughs and smiles. It is no surprise that when he retired, the students at Galena Elementary drew pictures of Mr. Perkins with one consistent feature, a huge smile. It may be a cliché, but that makes it no less accurate when we say that students will care what we know once they know how much we care.

Work as if nothing is beneath you

It was nothing for my dad to stay late after school-wide functions to make sure everything was cleaned up. When he had a student whose wheelchair made it difficult for her to disembark from the bus in the morning or board it in the afternoon, he was there to carry her. He spent the lunch period in the cafeteria when many other principals swore they would never set foot in such a place. It makes me think of the perhaps apocryphal story of Abraham Lincoln. An aide saw him blacking his boots and admonished him, "Sir, Presidents do not black their own boots." Without missing a beat, Lincoln replied, "Then whose boots do they black?" I hope I never think I am too good to pick up a piece of trash in my school.

Pay what you owe

My dad was responsible for making out the deposits for the milk money and the lunch money each week at his school. His accounts always balanced to the penny. When other principals talked of rounding things off, my dad would have none of it. Our family once went out to eat, and as we prepared to leave, my mom went to the restroom. Instead of paying, my dad and I began talking. We walked out without paying and without realizing it. Later that night, it hit my dad what had happened, and he made it a point to go back to that restaurant the next evening to pay our bill.

Support those around you

Galena Elementary was one of the first in our school district to make computers a regular part of instruction. This was in the late '70s and early '80s when the Apple II and the Apple IIe were the hot products. Computers were not exactly his thing, but my dad recognized their value and, more importantly, the passion and the ability of his teachers for whom computers were the thing. As one of them later told me, he supported them in their efforts to bring this technology into the school and encouraged them to help make Galena a cutting-edge school for its time.

I said that his work influenced many educators, and one of those was present the night the Floyd County commissioners passed their resolution on Norman R. Perkins Way. It was Donna Atwood, my dad's niece, and my cousin. Donna has done just about everything there is in the field of education, including drive a bus. She is currently the special needs coordinator at an elementary school in southern Indiana. That evening she told our children a bit of her story and what inspired her to become an educator. Not surprisingly, it had to do with an early childhood memory of visiting her Uncle Norman's school. I am sure my dad would say he had nothing to do with her becoming a teacher, but then again, that was just his way.

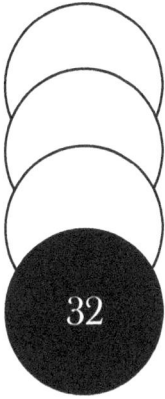

32 Call in the Experts

There was a time when teachers led students on field trips during which they could explore the world around them, often with the guidance of experts in a particular area. Those days are long gone for too many schools saddled with budgetary constraints that make trip transportation next to impossible. And while we do have the Internet and video access to vastly more information than we could explore *in situ*, these resources cannot replace the value of the human interaction that comes from having an expert interact with students in person. Primary and secondary teachers must reach out to university colleagues, and professors must ask their colleagues in the lower grades how they can help. By fostering relationships across the educational spectrum, we can retain a bit more of the humanity in the distinctly human enterprise that is education.

I shared once in an online education group some thoughts on student engagement based on the work of my Advanced Placement Latin students. My friend Dr. Betty Rose Nagle commented on this post, and that sparked a conversation between us that led to her coming to my school and speaking to my class.

Dr. Nagle is a professor emerita of Classical Studies at Indiana University.

With her focus on Latin and Roman studies, she translated Ovid's *Fasti* and the *Silvae of Statius*. She has also given many popular talks connecting the mythology of the ancient world with the mythologies of the modern day in comics and movies. With such a background, she was the perfect person to discuss with my A.P. Latin students the challenges, intricacies, and art of literary translation.

They asked her questions about translating from another language into Latin and whether her reading of other translations influenced her own work of translating the same author. She talked with them about her efforts in translating poetry using a more formal approach with iambic pentameter and a freer approach based on beats per line, and she even discussed the system of Roman metrics and how it was borrowed from Greek, a language to which it was much better suited than Latin.

And true to her own pedagogical roots, Dr. Nagle asked questions of the students. She asked them what they looked for in a translation, and their responses ranged from accuracy of content to literalness of grammar to flow to feeling. With each response, she spun the discussion deeper, bringing in at various points Frederick Ahl's *Aeneid*, the compilation of Ovidian translations called *After Ovid*, and Douglas Hofstadter's tome *Le Ton beau de Marot*, which addresses issues of literary translation by focusing on eighty-eight renditions of one tiny French poem.

For many years I used to take some of my students to visit the experts. The A.P. students made a trip each fall to Indiana University where they completed research at the undergraduate library, had lunch with a Latin professor, and then sat in on that professor's class.

We were also fortunate one year to have Dr. Bernard Barcio, former high school Latin teacher as well as adjunct professor of Latin at Butler University, visit one afternoon. He talked with the students about the catapult competitions he oversaw that became truly legendary in the 1970s, leading to numerous spots on ABC News.

Am I comfortable turning over my classroom to other teachers? I am, for it is important that students hear from different voices on the same subject. It is important for them to enter the realm of higher academic discussion before they enter a university. And it is important for them to see their teacher join them as a fellow student on the shared journey of discovery.

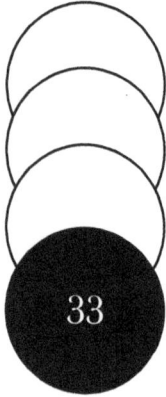

The Manual Capture of Moonbeams

33

This essay was written when I retired from public education.

Authentic teaching is a vocation. It is a calling.
George Steiner, *Lessons of the Masters*

I have no idea how to express what I feel as I plan to leave the school where I have taught for nearly a quarter century, the vast majority of my thirty-year career. There is no one I can ask to advise me on how to put these feelings into words. I could sooner get an answer to Rodgers's and Hammerstein's seemingly whimsical question, "How do you hold a moonbeam in your hand?" Then again, there is Pascal. *"Le coeur a ses raisons que la raison ne connaot point,."*[36] "The heart has its reasons that reason knows not of." And so, while Prufrock[37] may have wondered whether to eat a peach, I will not inquire how to convey emotion verbally. There is no Lucretian swerve[38] powerful enough to combine the alphabetic atoms into prose or poetry worthy of the task. Instead, let us consider why there should be such profound emotion connected with something as simple as retirement.

For thirty years I have taught Latin at either the middle school, high school, or undergraduate level. The most recent twenty-three have been at North Central High School in Indianapolis, Indiana. Brilliant colleagues with whom I conversed regularly about philosophy, art, language, science, world affairs, and politics made it a scholar's dream, yet it was the students, the insightful, intellectually curious, creative, and boundlessly energetic students who made this so much more than a mere job, and therein lies the first clue to why so much emotion has been caught up in my leaving.

"Authentic teaching is a vocation. It is a calling."[39] This observation from George Steiner's *Lessons of the Masters*, which is perhaps my favorite sustained treatise on education, starts us in the right direction. There are many forgeries in education, just as there are in any area of life. The cheap knockoffs display the trappings of teaching but are driven by formulas and fads and are given value only by inept instruments of testing. These are not our concerns here. Our interest is in authentic teaching, and of this Steiner goes on to say, "The teacher is aware of the magnitude and, if you will, mystery of his profession, of that which he has professed in an unspoken Hippocratic oath. He has taken vows."[40]

There is a religious cast to this, seen in words like "mystery," "oath," and "vows," and this is proper. Matters of faith and religion connect the human with the transcendent, and a teacher, no less than a priest, is a pontiff, which, as the Latin root *pontifex* reveals, is a bridge builder. Teachers help to connect students with ideas, with others, with themselves, and at times even with what lies beyond it all. How could a teacher not be aware of the magnitude of the profession, another word with religious undertones? Such work is sacred work, and just as one does not loudly and vulgarly stampede from a cathedral, one does not simply walk away from the place and people with whom he has engaged in such work.

I was stunned at the beginning of my career, as I am now, that I am paid to do what I do, and although I certainly support higher pay for teachers, there is something a bit odd about being paid at all. Steiner asks, "How can vocation be put on a payroll? How is it possible to price revelation? Why have I been remunerated, given money, for what is my oxygen and *raison d'être*? By what oversight or vulgarization should I have been paid to become what I am?"[41]

Stay with this for a moment. Yes, teachers must live and maintain a living, but when you consider the magnitude and mystery of what is really taking place when one teaches and another learns, does that truly seem something about which you can establish a monetary value?

Some will say that both Steiner and I are getting a bit above ourselves. After all, what we call teaching covers some rather mundane things, like teaching a child the alphabet or basic math facts, but I would counter that the authentic teacher never merely disseminates discrete pieces of knowledge. As Steiner puts it, "The choice...is between 'life' and the disinterested... pursuit of pure thought."[42]

Now we are getting somewhere. This is all about life. Education is a distinctly, indeed supremely, human endeavor. It is a shared journey of discovery. This is why Steiner can say that teaching is his "oxygen and *raison d'κtre*," as it has been mine. These students and I, we are all fearfully and wonderfully made,[43] and even in discussing the most simple or trivial of points, it is we, we human beings, who are doing the discussing. I should confess here that I would have been a failure as an administrator. Administrators are required by local statutes and state laws to evaluate teachers and students by criteria that, if not entirely meaningless, have less meaning for me. Yes, of course, students must leave a class knowing certain things, but the true evaluation of what has taken place in that class, which is to say the measure of the value that comes out of it, is life. Has what transpired, i.e., been breathed across, in the classroom given birth to or fostered the growth of life? And how would one know if it had? Ask yourself how you determine the life in anything. You see signs of it. In the life-bringing, life-giving classroom, you will find love, joy, happiness, curiosity, smiles, laughter, and the desire to discover and create. Such things do not fit well in a spreadsheet, and once again we are back to the manual capture of moonbeams.

In the annals of those teachers who have breathed forth life in and with their students, we typically recall the great figures of history or a dear teacher of our own. Rarely do we look to mythology and literature, and this is a sad consequence of how so much of our literature is taught today. We mine it for rhetorical features and agendas and ignore the role that story has always played, to teach and to edify, to warn and to model. Yet Steiner, for whom almost no literature was unfamiliar, finds the exemplary teacher in the centaur Chiron. "Half beast, half man, Chiron embodies wisdom when it is energy, the natural order when it branches, in dangerous beauty, into the human. He is the 'noble Pedagogue' *par excellence*. His pupils form a constellation like no other: Chiron has taught Orpheus, Jason and the Argonauts, Hercules, Asclepius, begetter of medicine. He has borne the child Achilles on his back. Chiron has educated 'for its glory a *Heldenvolk*,' 'a nation of heroes." What scholastic 'Magnificence' can be set beside the Centaur's?"[44]

Have you ever thought of teaching as the natural order branching in dangerous beauty into the human? Such a view sees teaching as far more than instructional strategies. Once again, we see life. There it is in nature and branching, which, as opposed to mere static branches, suggests growth.

Steiner cites the following as a creed of 19th century French philosopher and teacher Jules Lagneau. "[T]he only thing which can be fruitful is a living instruction, a teaching by and of the entire soul, of the whole person, of life."[45] Given that, can you wonder that my departure from such a long period of teaching among a particular group of people should cause me sorrow? Yet, it is time. I am retiring from North Central High School. Another will teach Latin here and, hopefully, strive to aspire to some of the vision of teaching that Steiner describes. That teacher will succeed in some areas and will fail in others, just as I have, but as Robert Browning reminds us, "a man's reach should exceed his grasp/Or what's a heaven for?"[46]

34 School is Not for Everyone

School is not for everyone, but education is. If that seems like a contradiction, then this essay is for you.

A colleague recently asked for my help in translating the Latin expression at the beginning of Silence Dogood's fourth letter, which she was using with her English class. If the name Silence Dogood sounds odd, it was the pseudonym Benjamin Franklin used to publish a series of letters that exposed the follies and absurdities of contemporary New England life, and in the fourth letter, published May 14, 1722, he took aim at schooling.

[A]s I pass'd along, all Places resounded with the Fame of the Temple of Learning: Every Peasant, who had wherewithal, was preparing to send one of his Children at least to this famous Place; and in this Case most of them consulted their own Purses instead of their Childrens Capacities: So that I observed, a great many, yea, the most part of those who were travelling thither, were little better than Dunces and Blockheads. Alas! alas!

I reflected in my Mind on the extream Folly of those Parents, who, blind to their Childrens Dulness, and insensible of the Solidity of their Skulls, because they think their Purses can afford it, will needs send them to the Temple of

Learning, where, for want of a suitable Genius, they learn little more than how to carry themselves handsomely, and enter a Room genteely, (which might as well be acquir'd at a Dancing-School,) and from whence they return, after Abundance of Trouble and Charge, as great Blockheads as ever, only more proud and self-conceited.[47]

That is rather strong stuff for our modern sensibilities that are so easily offended, yet he is right, and nothing much has changed in nearly three hundred years. School is no more suited for everyone than is the varsity football team or the concert orchestra, but because we have made of the diploma and the degree objects of worship, Franklin was correct in labeling the school a "Temple of Learning," and no parents want their children left in the outer darkness where there is much weeping and gnashing of teeth.

What matters most, of course, and what people truly desire is education, and education is attainable by any who want it from the company of those who know, and this need not always occur within a school. In fact, because the minimum requirements are the desire to learn and a source of knowledge, education can be gained by a solitary person surrounded by the best minds of humanity as they have expressed themselves in books, and indeed this has been the way many have acquired their education across the centuries. I would argue that the experience is better and more delightful and the resulting education deeper and richer when it takes place in a community of learners, but even this does not necessarily mean a school.

Take, for example, an observation by one of the fourth century Cappadocian church fathers, Gregory of Nyssa. He notes that at that time, everyone was discussing matters of the deepest philosophy and theology everywhere.

"For all parts of the city are filled with such things, the alleys, the crossroads, the marketplaces, streets, the clothes merchants, the money lenders, and those who sell food. If you should ask anyone the price, he would philosophize about the nature of the begotten and the unbegotten. If you inquire about the cost and value of bread, he says that the Father is greater and the Son subject to Him. If you say that the bathhouse is open, he states his opinion that the Son does not exist from things that already exist."[48]

To be fair, Gregory does not think terribly highly of this, but consider for a moment what he has described. Normal people are discussing some pretty heady stuff in the midst of everyday life. Yes, they had to have heard of such ideas somewhere, and that somewhere would have been the church, but these were not scholars at the academy. They were regular, likely unschooled; folks.

The point is this. Education is vital, for it equips a person to lead the richest possible life. Certain topics, or certain levels within such topics, are best approached in a formal environment like a school. Yet not everything of value needs to be learned there nor is always learned best there. Poetry, philosophy, theology, history, art, music, and the wonder of the sciences and mathematics, can be experienced and explored in other communities, even if that community consists of one living person and a great cloud of witnesses from across time in the pages of books. While we would be, rightly, loath to call students today dunces and blockheads, we would do well to help our children find the environment where they can best attain a true education, recognizing that it may not be in a school.

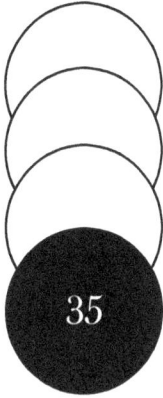

35 A Constitutional Education

On Monday, February 10, 2014, I was honored when Representative Eric Turner, Speaker Pro Tempore of the Indiana House of Representatives, brought forward a resolution recognizing me as the 2014 Indiana Teacher of the Year. After Representative Turner read the resolution, I was allowed to address the chamber, and what follows is the text of my remarks.

I want to thank the Honorable Eric Turner, Speaker Pro Tempore and House Member for the 32nd district, along with all the members of the Indiana House of Representatives for the opportunity to be with you today. When I was a senior in high school twenty-seven years ago, I could not have imagined returning to this chamber to speak to this body. In 1987 during my last year at New Albany High School in Floyd County, Indiana, we had the opportunity to take a regular government class or one called "TV-Government." I chose the latter and was able to travel to Indianapolis to film a program that involved interviewing members of the Senate and House of Representatives and State Superintendent of Public Instruction H. Dean Evans. My friend, Rick Wilson, was the cameraman and took footage of our handsome statehouse, and I remember returning home to New Albany convinced that I wanted to run for office. Now, nearly thirty years later, I teach at North Central High School in Indianapolis. Our administration building is named for H. Dean Evans, who was our district's superintendent before leading the state, and I am once again in a chamber that inspires me.

It is often said that obtaining a good education has never been more important than it is right now. This is only true because obtaining a good education is just as important now as it has ever been. Around 380 B.C. Plato wrote his famous *Republic*, a philosophical dialogue that tries to explore the ideal state. For Plato it was only natural to devote two chapters to the topic of education, for as he observed, matters of education are linked to matters of justice and injustice. He goes on to lay out a program of study that addresses the three parts of a human being, the body, the mind, and the soul. Plato knew that any curriculum that fails to address the complete person must fall short not only in preparing that person for all he or she could become, but in laying the foundation for a just state.

Hoosiers have known this as well. Our first constitution of 1816 listed as our primary purpose the establishment of justice. Article 9, Section 1 of that original constitution followed more than two thousand years of shared human understanding linking education and justice by proclaiming, "Knowledge and learning generally diffused, through a community, being essential to the preservation of a free Government, and spreading the opportunities, and advantages of education through the various parts of the Country, being highly conductive to this end, it shall be the duty of the General Assembly to provide, by law, for the improvement of such lands...for the use of schools, and to apply any funds which may be raised...to the accomplishment of the grand object for which they are or may be intended."[49] In Article 8, Section 1 of the current Indiana Constitution, we read, "Knowledge and learning, generally diffused throughout a community, being essential to the preservation of a free government; it shall be the duty of the General Assembly to encourage, by all suitable means, moral, intellectual, scientific, and agricultural improvement...."[50]

Times change, but truth does not. From 4th century B.C. Athens to 21st century Indiana, human beings have known that a just state is rooted in and supported by education, which, as Plato described, must be nothing less than the development of the whole person.

At North Central High School, I teach Latin, which is a microcosm of a complete liberal arts education, for in it we teach the whole child by including math, art, geography, history, English, and performing arts. Whether we are marching drills as the Roman soldiers did or creating wax tablets and scrolls as we explore ancient handwriting, the study of Latin opens the door to a world of endless fascination and discovery, and we connect the exciting world of education with issues of justice from the beginning. We take as our foundation a statement by the great Roman orator Cicero. "Let others be ashamed if they have so hidden themselves in literature that they can offer nothing from their reading for the public benefit nor can bring forth anything into the light to be seen."[51] This has led us to two annual projects, one to fight poverty in Indianapolis and another to help children at Riley Hospital. It has also inspired a new effort this year to build a literacy garden at a local elementary school.

My 7th grade English teacher, Dale Richmer, had a poster in his room that said, "The road to success is marked with many tempting parking places." We must resist the temptation to reduce education to nothing more than skills training. We must resist the temptation to see education as merely a ticket to a high-paying job. Education, of course, includes preparation for a career, but those who founded the state of Indiana knew and codified the idea that education is much more, a grand object, as they called it. I encourage each member of this House of Representatives and indeed all Hoosiers to remember the high ideal of what a well-rounded education can be, one that addresses the bodies, minds, and souls of our citizens. It is the type of education that led me to this chamber nearly thirty years ago when I was a student, and it is the kind of education that continues to flourish in many schools across our state, as it must if we are to remain true to our original charter of establishing justice. All Hoosiers must work to promote this deep and broad understanding of education, which is nothing less than the most humane and human of enterprises. Thank you.

Whenever one person leads another from the darkness of ignorance in any area to the light of understanding, it is a grand endeavor, one harried by threats as fierce as those found in our epic literature. Miscommunication constantly threatens misunderstanding, and attacks from illness, laziness, poor preparation by both student and teacher, emotional stress, hunger, exhaustion, and countless other sources make any success something of a miracle, and so the very process of teaching and learning makes education a grand object.

What we are aiming at in education is grand as well, for it is nothing other than the expansion and enrichment of a human mind. Cicero wrote,

Indagatio ipsa rerum cum maximarum tum etiam occultissimarum habet oblectationem. Si vero aliquid occurrit, quod veri simile videatur, humanissima completur animus voluptate.[52]

"The investigation itself of very important and at the same time quite obscure matters holds pleasure. If indeed it happens that something like the truth is discovered, one's spirit is filled with a most human pleasure."

Seen from this perspective, education is about much more than skills training or equipping someone for a job, however worthwhile that job or the mere fact of having a job may be. Only when we have glimpsed the grandness of the enterprise on which we are entering are we prepared for the magnificent rewards and challenges of true education.

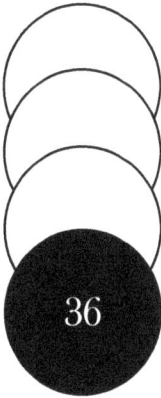

36 Spending Time with Euripides

It all started when my colleague at another school shared a recent article about Emily Wilson's new translation of the *Odyssey*.[53] Eric Leveque, who holds both a Bachelor's and a Master's degree in Classics, was observing me as part of his Transition to Teaching program at Indiana University, and I eagerly shared the article with him at the beginning of our planning/lunch period. We began an intense discussion about translation...the art of it, why people continue to engage in it, and the tantalizing impossibility of it. Before long we were deep into a discussion that took in the incarnation of Christ, the nature of eternity, Protestant and Catholic theology, symbolism and realism, the essence of liturgy, the essence of the Eucharist, the distinction between τὸ ἕν, the one, of Plotinus and ὁ ὤν, the one who is, that defines the God of Christianity, and what it means for high school students to enter into a text.

Both Eric and I can become quite distracted from more quotidian matters, and since he had not brought lunch, he had told me earlier of his need to run over to the local fast-food restaurant to grab something. Suddenly I realized that time was slipping by, but rather than end our stimulating conversation, I rode with him on his burrito quest simply to keep the discussion going. As he paid for his order, I posted quickly online about the joy of our conversation, and a friend soon replied, "Wow. I would love to get a degree in Classics."

And that comment takes us back to the article that started the whole thing. Wyatt Mason, the author of the article on Emily Wilson and her translation, wrote when describing her educational background, "[T]he appeal of classics as a discipline was profound." Why would that be? Why would the study of the literature and history, the cultures and languages, of the ancient Greeks and Romans offer a profound appeal? Why would my online friend say that she would love to get a degree in such studies?

Wilson's own story provides the answer, as Mason writes. "Although Wilson was undecided on a direction after taking her undergraduate degree – she had thoughts of doing law – she ultimately chose to do further studies in English literature at Oxford while she figured her way forward, rereading some of her favorite books, particularly Milton's *Paradise Lost*. Emerging with a sense that the writers she admired most were in dialogue with antiquity, Wilson pursued a Ph.D. in classics and comparative literature at Yale. Wilson knew that if she was 'being smart,' she ought to focus on something understudied, like Plutarch. 'I loved Plutarch, but I didn't love him as deeply as I loved Sophocles, Euripides, Milton. I just felt like I wanted to spend a little bit longer with Euripides.'"

I would not trade my B.A. in Classical Studies from Indiana University or my M.A. in Classics from The University of Texas for all the fish in the sea, and for the same reason that Wilson chose the direction she did. Studying, engaging with, entering into the thoughts and linguistic artistry of the ancient Greeks and Romans are not only supremely satisfying *per se*, but such pursuits initiate an infinite, expanding spiral of exploration into the greatest achievements of humanity. I can directly trace my fascination with and enjoyment of quantum physics, albeit at a layman's level, philosophy, poetry, cognitive science, prose, politics, and art to my Classical studies, and often these other interests have taken me back to the ancient world, for it is indeed true that many of the best of our thinkers and creators have been "in dialogue with antiquity."

If this were merely a piece describing a scintillating discussion with a colleague, I could just as well have left it as a blog post, yet there is more going on here. It is precisely Wilson's desire to "spend a little longer with

Euripides" and the wish of my friend to attain a degree in Classics that is the reason Eric and I and so many others have chosen to teach. We want others to experience such desires and wishes. We want to introduce them to the wonders of the ancient world that themselves become gateways to wonders yet undiscovered.

As Eric and I discussed, teaching, too, is translation. The *Aeneid* my students encounter is not the same as the one his students will experience, for he and I are unique human beings, and we will each bring to our presentation our own understandings. Yes, we will try to help our students read the great works for themselves, but even if they were to read in utter silence without our guidance, they would be performing their own interpretive act, making the translation of their reading a unique one. The best classroom, then, is not one in which students merely acquire knowledge, but one in which they enter into that which they study, becoming a part of it as it becomes a part of them. When that happens, students desire to spend a little bit longer with the authors and works that have shaped the world, and it is then that a teacher can say, "This is what I came to do."

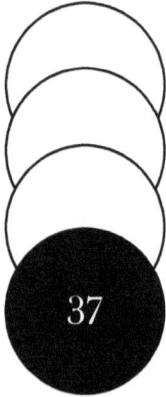

Reading, Warfare, Students, and Love

In the spring of my senior year of high school, my Latin teacher Marcene (Holverson) Farley made me aware of scholarship opportunities from the Indiana Junior Classical League. One of the applications required an essay based on a favorite Latin quotation, so I picked one by Cicero, whom I had studied as a junior the previous year under Alice (Ranck) Hettle.

"Ceteros pudeat si qui ita se litteris abdiderunt ut nihil ex eis possint neque ad communem adferre fructum neque in aspectum lucemque proferre."[54]

"Let others be ashamed if they have so hidden themselves in literature that they can offer nothing from it for the common good or can bring forth nothing into the light to be seen."

That line had stayed with me and came to mind again years later when, as I was driving to school one morning in 2009, I had an idea. I had read once about a group of college students reading Homer's *Iliad* aloud in Greek and getting pledges as a fundraiser. Cicero's quotation and that article came rushing through my mind like two pieces of uranium-235 at Los Alamos, and the result was a powerful new idea. What if high school students read aloud one of the Greco-Roman epic poems to raise money in an effort to fight poverty?

Details quickly came together, and a student named Brent Eickhoff introduced me to Shirley Mullin, owner of Kids Ink Bookstore in Indianapolis. She agreed to host our event and dedicated space in her front window where the students could sit to read. Zoe (Smith) Crafton, another student, designed a logo for us that we used on t-shirts for the readers and on a banner to advertise what we called Reading the War on Poverty, or RTWOP.

That first year saw Latin students from North Central High School reading aloud the entirety of Homer's *Iliad* in English translation. With the money they raised and a donation from the bookstore from that day's sales, we were able to give more than $1000 to Shepherd Community Center,[55] whose mission is to help break the cycle of poverty in Indianapolis. The event was so successful that we wanted to do it again, and Shirley and her staff at Kids Ink were pleased to help.

The following year our Latin students read Homer's *Odyssey*, the year after that Vergil's *Aeneid*, and the fourth year started the cycle over with the *Iliad*. Each year saw them raise more than $1000 for Shepherd, and RTWOP quickly became a flagship event in our Latin program.

In April of 2017, I was listening to students read the *Aeneid* in our ninth RTWOP and began thinking of what we could do to celebrate our tenth anniversary in 2018. People had often asked if we would read one of the epics in its original language, so we decided to break our repeating three-year cycle to read the *Aeneid* again the following year, but in Latin. More ideas developed, and we decided that RTWOP 10 would feature

- students reading in Latin
- a microphone and speaker to project the reading outside the store
- an invitation for alumni to participate with current students
- a commemorative edition of the *Aeneid* to give each reader
- the goal of raising $10,000

That last feature was by far the most ambitious, so we started an online funding campaign to help. Within minutes of launching it, we started receiving donations, and as the 2017-2018 school year progressed, we dared to hope we might actually reach our goal.

The next, fairly ambitious part of RTWOP 10 was producing a commemorative edition of the *Aeneid*. There are many editions available, but I wanted something special, something personal for the readers, and the only way to get that was to produce it myself. I used a version that was in the public domain and formatted the text throughout the summer and fall of 2017 and the winter of 2018. For the front cover I used a t-shirt design created by one of my students, Alexandria Ruschman, and included Zoe Crafton's original logo on the back along with our logo for North Central Latin, which had been created years before by my sister-in-law, Melanee (Stillions) Habig. My son, Austin, helped with the cover design, and I added a preface that concluded, "I could say regarding my pride in all my students what Jupiter said in *Aeneid* I.278 of the achievements that would come from the Romans, '*His ego nec metas rerum nec tempora pono.*' I set neither limit nor time to it."

Far less daunting was assembling the readers. RTWOP had become a much-anticipated event in our classes, and the reading times always fill up quickly. I had established an alumni group online and through it was able to invite former students. Twelve alumni eagerly signed up, and the remaining spots were filled with current first- through fifth-year students. A small army of fifty-nine readers would read in fifteen-minute shifts for four hours on a Friday evening and eleven more on Saturday. From the money they would raise, along with the online contributions and a donation from Kids Ink, we hoped to reach our $10K goal.

One of my stock lines in class is, "But wait! There's more!" and indeed there was. Shirley at Kids Ink reached out to her business neighbors up and down Illinois Street, and many of them decided to help as well. Eight businesses joined Kids Ink in supporting RTWOP in a variety of ways.

And then there was the social media campaign. For a full year there were social media posts promoting what we were doing, and there were two, true highlights, but to understand why they were so special, you need to know something about me. In the words of Joan Jett, "I love rock 'n' roll!" In fact, for a number of years I published a blog called *The Roman Rocker* and am the co-host of a Christian rock and metal podcast called *The Wildman and Steve Show*.[56] Classic rock, hard rock, and metal are what I love, so I was beyond thrilled when Michael Sweet, the lead singer of Stryper, shared the project to nearly 76k social media followers and David Coverdale of Whitesnake, who has 218k followers, liked one of our posts.

When the weekend finally arrived for RTWOP 10, the students and I were quite excited. The weather was beautiful, and blue sky, white clouds, and temperatures in the 70s guaranteed many people would be out in the delightful neighborhood of Illinois Street. From 4:00-8:00 p.m. on Friday, April 27, and from 9:00 a.m.-8:00 p.m. on Saturday, April 28, current Latin students and alumni read the *Aeneid* aloud in Latin. That ancient language was heard along Illinois Street as it was broadcast through our speakers, and people took notice. Many customers came in, eager to learn more about the event, and almost all gave a donation.

Pride, joy, overwhelming satisfaction in the achievement of students... these come nowhere close to describing how I felt and continue to feel. Can you even imagine what it was like to see students using their learning to benefit others this way? Before telling how it all ended, I want to say a word about the alumni who dropped by. In addition to my twelve former students who read, including three who had read in the inaugural event ten years before, other alumni stopped in just to say hi and to support what was going on. With all of them it was a thrill beyond words to hear stories about what they had studied after high school, where they were working, and developments in their families. Two of my former students had married each other, and two others were dating. One was a Classical Studies major at my alma mater Indiana University and hoped to be the first woman to translate the *Iliad*, *Odyssey*, and *Aeneid* into English. And one young man was excited to tell me he had achieved his dream of joining his father as a firefighter with the Indianapolis Fire Department.

When all was said and done, North Central Latin students had helped raise $12,455.34 to help fight poverty in their city. Some of our club officers as well as Indiana Junior Classical League state officers who attended North Central presented the check to Steve DeBuhr and the good people at

Shepherd Community Center on the last day of school, May 24, 2018.

If you have read this far, you know two things. You know both what amazing things students can do and are doing to use their education for the betterment of others and how incredibly proud I am of all of them.

38 My Friend, Yosef Cohen

"God don't make them any better. And that's a fact." So said Brigadier General Lewis Armistead of Major General Winfield Hancock in the film *Gettysburg*. Of all the words in all the literature I have read, these are the ones that come to mind upon the passing of my friend, Yosef Cohen. They come to mind quickly in association with him, for I have said them often over the years when speaking of him to others.

In 2012, Yosef, or Yossi as so many knew him, was honored by the Bureau of Jewish Education. In the video associated with that award,[57] you get a sense of who he was as an educator, and but as his colleague who for many years taught in the room next to his, I was blessed by something more, but let us start with educator.

As a teacher of Latin and occasionally Greek, I sometimes had questions about Hebrew, for that ancient language so often was intertwined with those of my discipline, Classics. The moment I even began to ask him a question, Yosef would suggest that we meet over lunch. We each brought out our lexicons, and the richest, headiest of conversations would begin, allowing me in a small way to count myself as one of his students.

He was also my interlocutor on matters of politics, the economy, education, world issues, and history. Our conversations during passing periods made me want to be late for my own classes so the discussions with Yosef could continue. He thought deeply and broadly, and this allowed him to bring civility to our conversations the likes of which many would think was no longer possible. With his passing, it very well may not be.

He played a paternal role for me as well, often pointing to his gray hair and my lack of it, perhaps being willfully blind to the increasing salt in the pepper of my beard. He cared for my wife and my children, asking about them after we returned from every school break and especially after summer vacation, and was genuinely concerned about my future. His advice was always sage, and it always, always aligned exactly with whatever my wife would say. I sometimes wondered if they talked behind my back so their counsel would agree.

His humor was legendary, and I rarely took my leave of him without hearing a new joke from his seemingly endless treasury. He lightened our department meetings with that humor and reminded us all that as important as teaching was, the business of schooling was far less so.

Children often have their heroes, real or imagined, that they delight in imitating, but it is rare for an adult to have, or at least to admit to having, such a model. My wife can testify that I have said many times over the years that I would like to be more like Yosef Cohen when I grow up, and in this I know I am far from alone.

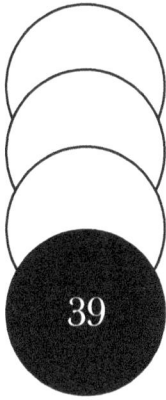

Bad Administrators Are Killing Education

39

Perhaps more than any other single factor, bad administrators are killing education. There are, of course, countless examples of excellent school administrators. I have known school principals and assistant principals who treated the teachers in their buildings with respect, who were quick with a compliment, and whose presence in a classroom teachers genuinely enjoyed. Yet there are far too many of the other kind, so I will say it again. Perhaps more than any other single factor, bad administrators are killing education.

That is a bold statement when the ability to educate our young people is under assault from poverty, poor home situations, a runaway obsession with testing, the misuse of data, blind worship of technology that in some cases brings more harm than good, and insulting attempts to make educators feel like professionals instead of allowing them actually to be professionals with appropriate salaries and control over how they practice their craft. Yet the ham-fisted, utterly misguided, and at times cruel leadership at district and building levels has produced "the most unkindest cut of all," leaving too many teachers with the choice of either crying, "*Et tu, Brute*?" to those who should have had their backs instead of stabbing them, or leaving the profession.

I once shared an article online, one more in a seemingly endless series of its kind, about a good teacher leaving the profession. This was not a new teacher who got in over his head or an older teacher who left because she was burned out. I sarcastically suggested in my preface to the post that there was no problem in teachers leaving, for, as some administrators say, there are plenty to take their place. I had no idea the hornet's nest I had poked.

In the days that followed, social media messages and emails bombarded me with stories from around the country of teachers bearing witness to hearing what is quite possibly the stupidest line of thinking that should get any leader fired for speaking it. Please note that the stories you are about to read must remain anonymous. I will give no indication of any teacher's name, subject matter, or state, and that alone is a matter worthy of concern, because the prevailing emotion in so many of our toxic school environments is fear. Teachers are afraid, and it is not because they are emotional snowflakes who need to grow up. It is because too many administrators, far from doing their job of fostering an environment in which teachers can do theirs, have created, whether through ignorant neglect or genuinely malevolent intent, a sweatshop mentality, complete with dread of the overseer's whip. It should not need to be said, but it must be. Fear is completely incompatible with education.

After a few responses to the article mentioned above, I asked whether educators had heard administrators say that there were plenty of teachers to take the places of those who leave, or a variant of that. The results were as follows, and there is no pattern of their coming from certain geographic regions or from one type of school or district over another:

Not comfortable responding to your [online] post, however, our HR Director told us in negotiations "...that there is a line of teachers waiting to take [our] place."

Teachers talk about administrators feeling that way; colleagues have throughout my career.

I've had it said to me two minutes before I was supposed to start teaching for the day.

At a new teacher hire, I heard, "With all due respect, as Beyonce says, 'Don't you ever for a second get to thinkin' you're irreplaceable.'"

I've heard it as well, multiple times and once through my own experience.

It makes me sad to say, but yes I have heard that at least once a year during my 15 years as a teacher.

Regrettably, I've heard it. I heard it said of some of the best educators with whom I have worked or co-taught.

On more than one occasion, I've heard a district administrator...state, "If they [teachers] don't like it, there are plenty of openings at McDonald's." Also, a district administrator...sent an email to a colleague with a link to a job opening in a neighboring district after she pointed out the potential impact of budget cuts on her department. It has been an interesting few years to say the least. It is one thing to deal with external perceptions of education and teachers; it's another when it is from within, especially from those in "leadership" positions.

"Everyone's replaceable" has been spoken many times in my school.

Quote at a school board meeting when a good young teacher decided to switch schools, "There is no one who can't be replaced."

Spoken by the principal to a colleague and me in his office when we told him about ill-will among the faculty, "When they leave, we will cry for three minutes and get back to work. I have a long list of people wanting jobs."

I've heard it in [name of state].

Yep, in [name of state] *I've heard it.*

A former superintendent used to say that – she used to say that teachers should be grateful for the jobs they have because there are lots of people lined up waiting to take them.

I've heard it several times in my own district and others in [name of state]. *It's so disheartening. We have so many vacancies.*

One of many reasons I moved into administration. I have heard it across the state in several districts.

I've heard it – especially at negotiation time.

I've sadly heard it when I taught in [name of state] *and a few years ago back in* [name of state].

My superintendent said a couple years ago that English teachers are a dime a dozen.

It's said regularly.

If you are a parent, talk to your children's teachers and administrators and find out for yourself the true culture of their school, making sure to encourage those leaders who are serving well. If you are in a university school of education, visit some schools in your state and discover for yourself their culture and then set yourself to the task of crafting leadership training programs capable of producing the leaders our children and teachers need. If you are a teacher, work well with your administrators. Lead up by sharing good leadership materials with your department chairs, principals, and superintendents. Encourage them when they do well. And if the environment of your school or district is such that you cannot be the teacher you were made to be, do not leave the profession, but find another place where you can thrive. The power of Pharaoh was broken by the exodus.

It is certainly the case that teachers who are not effective either need assistance to become better or need to leave the profession. Too much is at stake with the education of human beings for it to be mishandled by those who do not know how or do not care to shape and lead it properly. Yet when veteran teachers with proven records of success share such statements about their administrators, then surely "something is rotten in the state of Denmark."[58]

Whoever you are, as you go about the shared work of ensuring our children are well grounded in the past and present for their callings in the future, allow this extended email from a colleague of mine to motivate you:

It was via email, and regarding an extracurricular position I held. I have done this position for years, and the district has been very pleased with how I managed it, having brought it back from kind of a mess, thanks to my insane organization. However, it's a ton of work and for several years I've been feeling tired of being taken advantage of and tried to give it up.

This year there were some particular concerns I was raising, ethical concerns about some other staff members' conduct. When I approached admin about the fact that I wanted to give up my position, I told him I was concerned about handing it over to someone not as conscientious of the potential issues, as they've had difficulty getting the position adequately filled in the past, and I wanted to make sure to leave it in good hands because the integrity of the program meant a great deal to me.

Rather than addressing my concern he said, "Do the position or don't do the position. If you don't, someone else will" (paraphrase... I'm uncomfortable using his exact quote, but he did use the word *replaceable*). My immediate response was that he'd just made my decision really easy, and I emailed him back and said I wouldn't be doing it anymore.

This was said via email, at 7:28AM, as my 11th graders were walking in the door. I stood up to start class and as I was going over the agenda I just broke down. I had to excuse myself and took a couple of minutes to calm down. I told them,

"I'm sorry, something just happened that really upset me, and it has nothing to do with you."

There are a few things to this:

1) The fact that it was said in response to me raising concerns... it felt like he was saying "we'll find someone who's not going to raise a fuss" and it discounted all the heart and soul I'd put into the program for six years and trying to do the right thing.

2) While on the surface it's a logical and true statement, it's certainly not a great way to get your people to want to pour their heart into something that has few extrinsic rewards.

3) Our school has a major "positive school culture" initiative. Our principal is a driving force behind it, and goes out of his way to do special things and make it a positive environment. In many ways, he's wonderful at that task. But when he gets stressed out in the spring, he lashes out at people... and oftentimes he lashes out at his best people, the ones who are going above and beyond, the ones who are truly giving their all. But those day-to-day interactions mean just as much, if not more, than all of the positive murals and pep talks and recognitions and assemblies. I suspect he said it out of frustration with something that probably had nothing to do with me, but that's not an excuse, and I will never forget how worthless and unappreciated it made me feel that morning. I don't think I will ever have an interaction with him not colored by that experience.

40 A Heritage of Teaching

2016 saw Indiana celebrate its bicentennial, and as part of that celebration, Hoosier teachers shared stories of the educational heritage in their families. My family's Hoosier education heritage stretches back to the late 1800s and has continued nearly unbroken to this day. Since the Stoic philosopher and Roman emperor Marcus Aurelius devoted a significant part of his *Meditations* to naming the people who had influenced his life, I am dedicating this essay to my family of teachers.

On my mother's father's side of the family, our story begins with my great grandmother, Flora Carlile, who was born in 1862 and taught in a one-room schoolhouse in Washington County. Five of her children continued as teachers, including my great uncle Edwin Carlile (b. 1886), who taught wood shop at Froebel High School in Gary; my great aunt Bessie Pearl Carlile (b. 1893), who taught in a one-room schoolhouse and then the consolidated Finley Township School in Scott County; and my great aunt Goldie Ethel Carlile (b. 1896), who taught in a one-room schoolhouse in Scott County and then for 41 years at State Street School (renamed Lillian Emery Elementary School) and Silver Street School in New Albany; and my great aunt Myra

Jean Bailey (b. 1899), who taught in the 1920s in a one-room school in Scott County. Her daughter, Phyllis Anne Thompson (b. 1927), taught English at Scottsburg High School in the 1940s and 1950s, and Anne Thompson's son-in-law, Joe D. Smith (b. 1946), taught English and served as librarian for 37 years at Scottsburg High School and Scottsburg Middle School.

Flora's youngest child was my maternal grandfather, James Hanley (*sic*) Carlile. Born in 1906 and named after Indiana Governor James Franklin Hanly, he taught in a one-room schoolhouse in Scott County in the 1920s and 1930s.

On my mother's maternal side of the family, her cousin Ottis Ivan Schreiber (b. 1921) served as professor and department chair of English at Eastern Michigan University in Ypsilanti.

With such an educational bloodline, it was not surprising that my mother, Patricia Lee Carlile (b. 1937) wanted to become a teacher. Further inspired by her own second-grade teacher, who captivated her attention in the mid-1940s with the first pair of red shoes she had ever seen and then drove her when she was a senior for a visit to what then was Indiana State Teachers College (now Indiana State University), my mother earned a B.S in Education from Indiana State and later an M.S. from the University of Wisconsin. She taught fourth grade from 1959-1968 at Mt. Tabor Elementary School in New Albany.

It was at Mt. Tabor that my mother met my father, Norman Ray Perkins (b. 1930), who taught sixth grade there after teaching sixth grade in Lake Fenton, Michigan (1957-1959). He had earned his B.S. in Education from Indiana University thanks to the G.I. Bill after returning from service in Korea and later earned his M.S. from the University of Michigan. After they married in December of 1967, my mother left teaching at the end of that school year. My father started in the fall of 1968 as the principal of Galena Elementary School in Floyd County and remained there until his retirement in 1992.

My wife, Melissa (Stillions) Perkins, and I have taught Latin in Missouri, Texas, and Indiana, she at elementary, middle school, and high school levels, and I at middle school, high school, and undergraduate levels. Based on this heritage of teaching in my family and my own experience of the joys of this calling, I have long claimed as my favorite scene in any movie the following from the 1966 film *A Man for All Seasons*, which is based on the play of the same name by Robert Bolt and tells the story of Sir Thomas More: in this scene a young friend of More asks him for help obtaining a position in the court of King Henry VIII of England. More knows that the young man lacks the character to withstand the temptations of court life but that as a scholarly person he would do well in academic life and advises him to pursue a position at the local school.

More:	You would make a fine teacher, perhaps even a great one.
Richard Rich:	And if I was, who would know it?
More:	You, your pupils, your friends, (*pause*) God. Not a bad public, that.

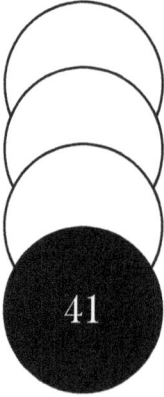

The Rise and Fall of Student Engagement

I told my Advanced Placement Latin students one day that they were a reason for getting up in the morning. Their emotion-laden response of, "Awwww! Mr. Perkins!" was sweet, but let us move past sentiment and on to the reason for my perfectly honest comment.

We were reading Vergil's *Aeneid* and had come to the part in Book I in which Neptune calmed the sea after a storm unleashed by Aeolus, god of the winds, had churned it into a maelstrom. In line 154 the great Latin poet wrote, "*sic cunctus pelagi cecidit fragor*," which literally comes into English as, "thus all the crashing of the sea fell." The key word in this tale I am about to tell is *cecidit*, a perfect tense form of *cadere*, meaning "to fall." Katie, a junior and one of our Latin club officers, suggested "subsided" for this word, but immediately said that this translation indicated a change over time, whereas the Latin word described something quick. I was stunned at her appreciation for such nuance and rewarded her with a piece of colored duct tape.

A short aside is needed here. Several years before, a student had said or asked something brilliant, and I wanted to acknowledge it with a small gift. Having nothing of value in my room, I ripped off a piece of gray duct tape from a roll I just happened to have with me that day and offered it as the award. It was something of a joke, but the students thought it was cool, and soon I began receiving rolls of the adhesive. We have had lime green duct tape, silver duct tape, and glow-in-the-dark duct tape with ghosts and bats. There has been tie-dyed, paint-splatter, and candy-striped duct tape, and receiving a piece of the stuff to put on a notebook has become the most desired achievement.

But back to the story. Katie had raised the issue of finding just the right word to translate something, and although we were a bit behind in our syllabus, it was a moment that could not be passed by. I distributed various translations of the *Aeneid* and instructed the students to find the passage we were reading. We then made a list on the board of the verbs that the translators had used to render *cecidit* into English.

And then the lid simply blew off. We talked about how "subsides" is present tense even though the Latin is perfect, but that such a translation is justifiable as a historic present. We discussed how three different translations chose "fell silent," retaining the basic sense of the Latin verb, yet adding the word "silent," and that this, too, is justifiable, for "to fall silent" is an English idiom. We observed that "abated" makes a one-verb to one-verb equivalency and maintains the perfect tense, and we talked about how "subsided," "died down," and "grew quiet" all contain a sense of change over time, just as Katie had observed about her initial suggestion.

I pointed out that they were all reasonable translations, and then I asked them which they preferred. Nicholas liked the single word "abated" and thought the sound and meaning perfectly captured the essence of *cecidit*. His peers thought some of the other translations worked better, although I do not think anyone preferred "subsides."

We laughed that our discussion of one verb had taken nearly half the class period, but by the time the bell rang, we were close to being back on track with our syllabus. Yet that was of little importance. Those students could appreciate the nuances and subtleties of translation and were eager to explore them. In their plumbing of the depths of a verb meaning "to fall," they rose to the heights of academic engagement.

42 Why I Love Teaching

It was #LoveTeaching Week across America. My friends Gary Abud, Jr. (2014 Michigan Teacher of the Year) and Sean McComb (2014 National Teacher of the Year), along with other state and national teachers of the year, were behind this project in which teachers all over the country blogged and posted to social media stories about why they loved teaching.

The education profession is frequently the subject of intense talk, and not all of it is positive. #LoveTeaching was an effort to cut through all that and take us directly to people. After all, teaching is a very human and humane enterprise. And since teaching is about people, I contributed to #LoveTeaching with thoughts about those who influenced me, my own teachers.

From kindergarten through graduate school, I was blessed to be a student of some of the finest educators. I thought so at the time because they were my teachers, and it is the natural state of affairs for children to love their teachers. After decades of teaching at the middle school, high school, and undergraduate levels, I can confidently say that I was right. These are the reasons I #LoveTeaching.

Mr. Goldstein taught sixth grade at Slate Run Elementary School in New Albany, Indiana. He prepared us as no one else could have for the world of higher learning we would encounter in junior high. He sparked and developed my love of writing, and I owe him a debt to this day.

Mrs. DeRungs was my high school choir director. I still find myself singing pieces from her choirs such as "Sicut Cervus," "Ave Maria," and "Ave Verum," even when I am going about the business of daily life. I remember once asking her what sort of shoes we should wear for an upcoming concert, and she remarked the gray ones I had would be perfect. I was stunned. She had seen me wear a certain pair of shoes and remembered. I make it a point today to comment on the clothes and personal items of my students because of her.

Jim Dickman was a brilliant force of nature. He taught me racquetball and Calculus, but more importantly, he modeled the life of the intellect lived out in the public square. Because he was a true master of his subject, mathematics, he was able to make it accessible to those just starting on its journey. I continue to talk with younger teachers about the importance of subject mastery for the effectiveness of teaching.

Simply put, I would not be doing what I am doing were it not for Miss Alice Ranck. Even though she retired at the end of my junior year to marry her high school sweetheart, she had already given me my life's direction. Were I to describe the full measure of her influence, this book would be too heavy to lift. She was a scholar and teacher of the first order, and there is not a day that goes by that her influence is not felt by the students in my own classroom.

Marcene (Holverson) Farley was my Latin teacher during my senior year, yet despite that I had her as a teacher for only one year, we successfully crossed the teacher-student boundary and enjoyed many conversations over the years as colleagues and even now in her retirement remain friends. While she was still teaching, rarely did a month pass in which we did not talk about education issues, she back in her native Illinois and I in Indiana. She has been one of my greatest champions and cheerleaders from high school, in college, and throughout my teaching career. She is a daily reminder and model to me of what true investment in the life of a child should look like, an investment I endeavor to repay in the lives of my own students.

Tim Long taught me Greek when I was an undergraduate and became my friend. It is as simple as that. While I will always remember his teaching me the foundations of Greek, it is his friendship that I cherish above all. I spent time in his office discussing heartbreak issues over the girl I was dating, and it was no surprise, but a great honor, when he attended our wedding a few years later. I see him almost every time I am in Bloomington, Indiana, and have consulted him countless times on Classics-related questions over the years. He regularly met with my students when we used to take an Advanced Placement Latin trip to Indiana University, and when he retired, we established a scholarship in his name at my high school. In ways my students will never know, he is teaching them every day.

Betty Rose Nagle taught the first and the last Latin classes of my undergraduate career. As a freshman I had her for Cicero and as a senior for Ovid. I will never forget her teaching me crucial aspects of how to write at the collegiate level during that freshman class, and today we remain friends. As a go-to person whenever I have a Classics question, she is the perfect example of the lifelong relationship between teachers and students.

Ellie Leach led me through the poetic works of Horace and Catullus, and through her I learned why certain (naughty) words were not listed in my dictionary! My wife was fortunate to have her as well, and when she attended our wedding, it was an honor. Even more striking to us was when she remembered us as we ran into her on campus years later. I was blessed a few years ago to give away one of my former students in marriage, having been asked by both her and her mother to do so, and I could not help thinking of Ellie and what it means for teachers to be deeply involved in the lives of their students.

Michael Gagarin taught my first graduate seminar in Classics, which was on the Greek Sophists, at The University of Texas. When he asked me to share in the seminar something I had written in one of my papers, I was flattered and overwhelmed. I had the great fortune of teaching his daughter later when she was in my high school Latin class in Austin, Texas, and when he spoke some years later at Wabash College in Indiana, I simply had to make the trip to see him.

I knew Bill Nethercut in two completely different ways. First, I knew him as my professor of Medieval Latin and then through his wife, Jane, who was my colleague as a high school Latin teacher in Austin. Bill brought the pure joy of life to his work as a teacher and scholar. He was constantly laughing and smiling, and it is that sort of atmosphere I strive to create with my students today. After all, Latin and Classics are part of the humanities, which means they are about people, and human endeavor should principally focus on life.

I wish I had pictures of all my teachers from kindergarten through graduate school. I can remember almost every one of them and have many stories to tell. Instead, I must settle for this listing of names. Although a few names escape me, such as the graduate assistants when I was an undergraduate, these are the teachers under whom I sat, from kindergarten through my final graduate school class. Each contributed one of the many reasons I #LoveTeaching.

Anne Roberson, Zelda Everbach, Maxine Dersch, Debbie Kimeck, Marcia Austin, Donald Dewey, Neal Lang, Irvin Goldstein, Jo Shaffer, June Gray, John Cutshall, Dale Richmer, Alice Jones, Carl Miles, James "Sonny" Wright, Charles Wolf, Sue Hughes, Cece Sher, Bob Jones, Lester Blank, Barbara Thrasher, Kathy Smith, Barbara Cannon, Ed Barnes, Doug Bierman, Bob Graves, Stephen McKinley, Connie Fleshman, Vern Ratliff, Keith Hofmeister, Bob Holman, John Silver, Joyce Woller, Dutch Vigar, David Runge, Dick Wardell, Jack Ford, Terry Austin, Bill Shofner, Linda DeRungs, Alice Ranck Hettle, John Buerger, John King, Phil Thrasher, Evelyn Cooper, Craig Flora, Evelyn Cooper, Fred Smith, David Grosheider, John Richardson, Jim Dickman, Jack Smith, Bob Dusch, Lee Kelly, Marcene Holverson Farley, Tim Long, Ted Ramage, Thomas Ehrlich, Betty Rose Nagle, Eleanor Winsor Leach, Martha Vinson, Louis Perraud, Hornfay Cherng, Elizabeth Steiner, Lorraine Strasheim, Andrew Riggsby, M. Gwyn Morgan, Gareth Morgan, Douglass Parker, Peter Green, Lesley Dean-Jones, Bill Nethercut, Paula Perlman, Michael Gagarin, and Paul Woodruff

Ideas From a Fifth-Grade Teacher

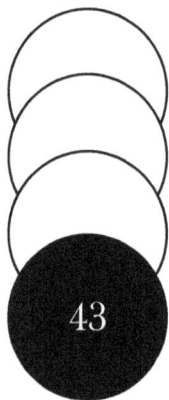

43

On May 24, 1980, I jotted down my top ten list of things I wanted to do as a teacher. It was the end of my 5th grade year, and I did not want to forget the ideas I had formed in Mr. Neal Lang's class at Slate Run Elementary School. The teaching bug had bitten me early, and Mr. Lang was everything I thought a professional, organized, educational leader should be. He required us to keep an assignment book in which it was our responsibility to write the homework that he had listed on the board each day for our various subjects. Even though this was still elementary school, his approach made me feel big and important, no longer a little boy who had
 to be spoon fed his assignments, and it turned out that my mother saved that list I had written.

As with many children, going to the doctor made me want to be a doctor, going to the dentist made me want to be a dentist, and the desire to be a teacher when I was in fifth grade was specifically the desire to teach that grade level. Some of my ideas from all those years ago were clearly related to teaching at the elementary level, such as having sign-and-return folders for student work, but others have made their way into my current high school Latin classroom. For example, the first idea on my list, "have a manila folder for each subject," plays out electronically. I have on my computer at school 8,601 files in 509 folders.

Although I do not lead my students in physical education every day (idea #10), we occasionally take a "walkabout" in which we walk around the school, pointing out and naming things in Latin. Why do we do that? We do it because sometimes students, and teachers, just need to get up and get the blood flowing again.

A no-comic-book policy (idea #3) has morphed into requiring students to put their phones away, at least during certain activities. My list of materials at the beginning of school asks students to bring some kind of writing utensil every day and a colored pen for marking assignments (idea #6). I do not list homework assignments on the board (idea #2), but put them on our web-based learning management system.

As I look back at the list I wrote in fifth grade, three things strike me. The first is idea #8, "have a good sense of humor." Not one period of one day goes by in which there is not considerable laughter in our room. We have fun with learning and fun with each other, and along the way a true culture of family grows among our Latin students.

The second idea that catches my attention is #9, "read to students every day." That idea was apparently so important to me in fifth grade that I underlined the word "every." I do not fulfill this in the classroom, but at home, when our children were little, I would read to them each night. It was always the best part of my day, and I enjoyed continuing the practice even as they grew older.

The third thing that strikes me about this list is the list itself. I have wanted to be many things over the years, some with more and some with less seriousness: author, public speaker, lead singer in a hair metal band, blues guitarist, and so forth. Yet at my core I am a teacher. I have been since kindergarten when I came home one day to find my grandma visiting, whereupon I gave her a quiz and gleefully marked everything wrong to give her an F. I have been since fifth grade when I began to get serious about planning for a life in education. I have been since high school when the pieces started to fall into place, and I knew that I would teach Latin. Teaching is not just what I do. It is who I am.

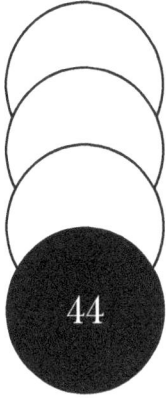

The Logic of Learning

If learning has not happened, has teaching taken place?

If the learner has not learned, the teacher has not taught.

These are variations on one of the most illogical notions to come down the pike. It may well be, as Bertie Wooster would be likely to say, the rummiest thing I've heard in a lifetime of rummy things.[59]

Definition: **necessary condition** – A necessary condition for some state of affairs S is a condition that must be satisfied for S to obtain.

Definition: **sufficient condition** – A sufficient condition for some state of affairs S is a condition that, if satisfied, guarantees that S obtains.

A simple undergraduate logic or philosophy class introduces these basic terms. Let me illustrate with an example.

Oxygen is a **necessary condition** for me to live. I must have oxygen to breathe. If I do not have oxygen, I cannot breathe and will die. Another way to say it is "without which not." Since without oxygen I would not live, oxygen is a necessary condition for my life.

Oxygen is not, however, a **sufficient condition** for me to live. There is plenty of oxygen in the morgue, and we do not see dead people jumping up to do the mambo. Another way to say it is "with which must." It is not true that with oxygen in the room a person must live. Oxygen, therefore, is not a sufficient condition for my life.

The absurdity of statements like, "If the learner has not learned, the teacher has not taught," is that they are based on the idea that teaching is a sufficient condition for learning, and this is not the case. Here are a few of the innumerable reasons why.

1. Teacher teaches, student gives outward indication of attention, student is thinking about the cute so-and-so two rows over.

2. Teacher teaches; student gives outward indication of attention; biological factors such as lack of sleep, lack of food, medical issues, and so forth, cause student not to remember

3. Teacher teaches; student gives outward indication of attention; social factors such as relational issues at school, abusive conditions at home, and so forth, cause student not to remember

4. Teacher teaches, student refuses to learn

The point is clear. It is entirely possible for a good teacher to teach well and for a student or even multiple students in the class not to learn. In fact, I will go so far as to say that teaching is not, according to the definition above, even a necessary condition for all learning. If it were, then no one could learn without a teacher teaching, and that is obviously not the case. No one needs to teach me that I will feel better if I put on a coat before going out in subzero temperatures. I can learn that just fine on my own by going out once or twice without one.

It is true, of course, that teachers and teaching are important. In many, perhaps even most, cases, teachers provide the most efficient means of learning something. There are even instances where teaching is, in a strictly logical sense of the phrase, a necessary condition for learning. For example, there is no way I am going to learn quantum mechanics without a teacher teaching me. Even then, it is no sure bet, but it is guaranteed not to happen without a very patient, kind, and knowledgeable physics teacher.

Yet it is simply not the case that teaching is a sufficient condition for learning. Does bad teaching make the learning more difficult? It certainly does. Can bad teaching stop learning entirely? It certainly can. What one cannot do, ever, anywhere, under any circumstances, is make the logical claim that because a student has not learned, teaching has not occurred. It may be true, mind you. A student may not have learned because teaching, or good teaching, did not occur, but that is not a conclusion you can logically draw solely from the lack of learning itself.

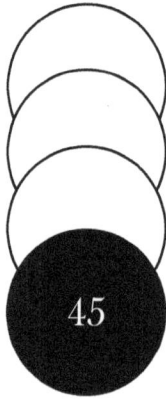

45 Fifty Minutes

It was a class like any other and because of that it was a class like no other. My third period class was second-year Latin, and we were finishing our study of Julius Caesar. The warm-up activity was to translate an English sentence into Latin. Following that, we read and discussed a passage of Latin poetry related to Caesar. On the surface this would not seem to be terribly exciting stuff.

Ah, but you were not there. The warm-up sentence was the most complex piece the class had seen. It was a compound sentence with two subordinate clauses, one of which contained a passive periphrastic. Yet the students had been completing prose composition exercises since the beginning of the semester and they were ready.

Using different colors, we analyzed the parts of the sentence first. We talked about the need to re-word the clause "troops must form a battle line" to read "a battle line must be formed by troops" so we could more easily construct the Latin passive periphrastic. The students then turned to their notebooks and began the task of composing the Latin.

I walked around the room, and the questions were simply astonishing.

"Why is 'was announced' passive, but 'was announcing' is active?" "Why does the form of the verb 'to be' need to be an infinitive?" "How do you find the stem to make the gerundive?" Again, these may seem rather ho-hum questions, but the earnestness with which they were asked and their specificity spoke volumes. These average, normal, typical teenagers were not throwing up their hands in despair. They did not simply check out and put their heads on their desks. They knew what they needed to know and were able to formulate the right questions to obtain that information. I am not exaggerating when I say that every single student was actively searching notes, figuring things out, and asking questions. Many came within two or three minor errors of perfection, and one young lady was just one letter off in one word.

From there we turned to our discussion of a passage from Book IX of Lucan's *Pharsalia*, an epic poem written in the first century A.D. about a battle between Caesar and Pompey in 48 B.C. Because our unit was primarily on Caesar's writings and since Lucan's poetry is quite challenging, we did not read the poem in Latin but from a bi-lingual version with Latin and English on facing pages. The passage we read that day gave Cato's speech to Pompey's men as they were about to face the arduous march back home across the inhospitable region of North Africa. We talked about Marcus Porcius Cato Uticensis and how his name has stood for two thousand years as the symbol of honesty and uprightness of character. We talked about Joseph Addison's 1713 play Cato: *A Tragedy* and why George Washington had it performed for his men on the eve of Valley Forge. Students asked questions like, "Why do we think of Caesar as a hero if a man like Cato was against him?" This, of course, led to a discussion of the complex nature of any person and how it is possible to admire and even imitate some qualities while being opposed to others. When we read Lucan's lines—

> *at, qui sponsore salutis*
> *miles eget capiturque animae dulcedine, vadat*
> *ad dominum meliore via*[60]

> *Must any soldier be assured of danger there's relief,*

So taken with life's sweetness, let him seek another chief—

we talked about how success is not always assured, a good grade is not guaranteed, and a job after college is not a given, but that a true leader will always shoot straight and not sugar coat things. The line "for whether I command or serve, I would not have it known" prompted the observation that the real leader is a servant-leader, serving alongside the rest.

It was fifty minutes of intense, complex, grammatical work and intense, complex, philosophical/historical discussion. Conversation with one young man even continued after class, and I think it is safe to say that this ordinary class of young people, some honor students, but many not, proved the truth of Cato's words, "True honor comes more joyful when at higher cost it's won."[61]

46 How to Start the School Year

I had never been so eager for the start of a school year. In particular, I could hardly wait to see my third-year, fourth-year, and fifth-year Latin students, for we would begin those upper-level classes with a plunge into one of the most thrilling experiences of my life. I had done something over the summer that I had longed to do for more years than my students had been alive. I was able to see and touch the one object in the world I had wanted to encounter more than any other. It related to their studies, and many of them knew about this passion of mine, so it was appropriate that I share it with them. Yet there was another reason why I would start the year with that experience. I will say more about that reason and the experience itself shortly, but for now, a bit of literary and historical background is necessary.

From 1715 to 1720, Alexander Pope published in six volumes his translation of Homer's *Iliad*. These six volumes were produced at great expense by Bernard Lintot and were sold by subscription to some of the most important names of the early 18th century. Pope arranged a deal for himself unheard of at that time for a writer and secured his financial future. A little later he published his translation of the Odyssey, but with the help of two uncredited poets named Fenton and Broome.

The *Iliad* had, of course, been published in English prior to Pope, most notably in by George Chapman in rhyming fourteeners in 1611 and heroic couplets by John Ogilby in 1660. Pope himself was taught to read by a loving aunt from the large, illustrated version by Ogilby.[62]

Since the *Aeneid* had been translated into English heroic couplets just a few years before by John Dryden, and because Pope's own literary star was on the rise, he was encouraged to take on Homer, and so he did. The great 18th century biographer Samuel Johnson, in his *Life of Pope*, said this of it. "It is certainly the noblest version of poetry which the world has ever seen; and its publication must therefore be considered as one of the great events in the annals of learning."[63] Consider the majesty of the opening lines of Book I from Pope's version.

Achilles' wrath, to Greece the direful spring
Of woes unnumbered, heavenly goddess, sing!
That wrath which hurled to Pluto's gloom reign
The souls of mighty chiefs untimely slain,
Whose limbs, unburied on that naked shore,
Devouring dogs and hungry vultures tore.
While great Achilles and Atrides strove,
Such was the sovereign doom, and such the will of Jove.[64]

Or consider these from Book V in which the acts of my favorite of the Greek warriors, Diomedes, son of Tydeus, are depicted with such raging force.

Thus toiled the chiefs, in different parts engaged;
In every quarter fierce Tydides raged.
Amid the Greek, amid the Trojan train
Rapt through the ranks, he thunders o'er the plain;
Now here, now there, he darts from place to place,

Pours on their rear or lightens in their face.
Thus from high hills the torrents, swift and strong,
Deluge the plains and sweep the trees along
Through ruined moles the rushing wave resounds,
O'erwhelms the bridge, and bursts the lofty bounds!
The yellow harvests of the ripened year
And flatted vineyards, one sad waste appear
While Jove descends in sluicy sheets of rain,
And all the labours of mankind are vain.
So raged Tydides, boundless in his ire,
Drove armies back, and made all Troy retire.[65]

I have collected a fair number of translations of Homer and Vergil, but Pope's version of the *Iliad* is still the one to get my blood pumping, and for years I had wanted to see a first edition of Pope's rendition. I had found them in rare bookstores on the Internet, but had never seen or held one in person until our family vacation one summer. We had stopped in Midtown Scholar,[66] a delightful bookstore in Harrisburg, Pennsylvania. It was enormous, with three floors of used, rare, and new books. I had ventured to the basement and, after perusing aisle after aisle, turned a corner into another store housed within the larger store. It was called Robinson's Rare Books and Fine Prints. Most of the works were in locked, wood and glass cabinets arranged by century. I asked the man working there if they had any Pope, and he checked his computer to find that they had a nine-volume set of his collected works, so I asked him to show it to me. As he was unlocking its cabinet, I spotted the volumes of Pope's *Iliad* and *Odyssey* nearby and asked if I could see one. I withdrew the first volume of the *Iliad*, nearly shaking and with my heart beginning to beat fast. I took it to a table where I could look at it and quickly opened to its frontispiece. My eyes raced down the page whose reproduction I had seen so often, and there I found the date, 1715. I was holding and looking at a first edition of my most sought-after book in the world.

I quickly called for my wife and children to join me, and our son took several pictures of me with the book. It was in astoundingly good shape for being exactly 300 years old, and I was thrilled to see the original opening lines that Pope changed for later versions.

The wrath of Peleus' son, the direful spring
Of all the Grecian woes, o goddess, sing!

I had had only one other experience like that with a book and, unsurprisingly, it was with another edition of Pope. When we were living in Texas, my wife and I visited a perfectly ordinary bookstore. I was perusing the Classics section, and suddenly my eyes lit upon a Penguin edition of Pope's *Iliad*. It was October 26, 1996, and I recorded the moment on a note I now use as a bookmark in that volume.

Ineffable was the feeling when by the grace of God I chanced upon this volume of Pope's Iliad. The edition is indeed nothing remarkable, and yet when I happened upon it quite by accident in the most commercial of bookstores, I was rendered truly senseless. My sense of balance lost, I was forced to support myself upon a nearby bookcase. Quite truly the sight of that volume, there, unobtrusively standing amidst other great works, whose bookshelf was itself surrounded by a sea of vain publications, "eripit sensus mihi: nam simul te, Papa, aspexi, nihil est super mi, lingua sed torpet, tenuis sub artus flamma demanat, sonitu suopte tintinnant aures, gemina teguntur lumina nocte."

The Latin lines are from Catullus 51, which the Roman poet wrote upon falling in love at first sight, albeit from across the room, with Clodia Metella. The only word I changed was the name of the addressee. "It snatches my senses from me, for as soon as I have laid eyes on you, Pope, there is nothing left for me, but my tongue grows numb, a slight flame runs down my limbs, my ears ring with their own pounding, and my eyes are covered with darkness."

This is what it means to say education is a shared journey of discovery. At the start of that school year, I wanted to kindle in my students the spark of learning's passion by drawing them close to my own burning flame. Those upper-level students knew of Greco-Roman epics, and the fifth-year Latin students had read Vergil. They knew of Pope and they knew of the challenges and the artistry of literary translation. They knew the excitement of discovery through archaeological finds and through their own experiences with Classical literature. It was important that they also knew their teacher was no less passionate and was in fact wildly excited about the field of their study. I could think of no better way to start the school year.

47

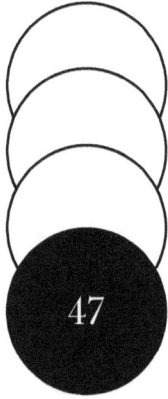

Do I Have to Like You to Teach You?

If we limit the definition of teaching to nothing more than giving information, then the answer is obviously no. A person who hates my living guts may shout, "That truck is about to hit you!" His motivation may be purely selfish. He does not want the truck to splatter my innards all over his new car. His tone could have been quite abrasive. Nevertheless, at the basest level, he has taught me something, namely that a truck was about to hit me, a fact of which I may not have been aware.

This, of course, is not what most of us mean by teaching. We have a general understanding that teaching involves someone who knows a thing and someone who does not. For any of a large number of reasons, they have been brought together, and the one who knows the thing must do something so the other person knows it, too. In this scenario, it is also not necessary that the teacher likes the student. The teacher can do a perfectly adequate job of imparting information so that the student acquires the intended knowledge or skill. During the teaching interaction, the teacher may well care nothing about the student, focusing solely on the paycheck to be received for teaching.

The teacher may even harbor ill will toward the student.

But let us take it a step further to genuine education. This is a far different enterprise. Genuine education is an infinitely complex activity that cannot happen apart from meaningful and intentional relationships. It is a distinctly human enterprise and therefore must be a humane one as well if it is to have any hope of success.

My friend Gary Abud, Jr., a Michigan Teacher of the Year, and I once co-hosted an education podcast, and one of our guests was Anne Marie Osheyack, the 2014 Massachusetts Teacher of the Year. What struck me most in her episode was her emphasis on the need to like students and to see them as human beings.

Sadly, this seems to be a novel concept. I say it is novel, for what I hear most regarding education has to do with curriculum, testing, teacher evaluations, data, school ratings, politics, standards, and taxes.

It is, of course, important to know something about our students, and there is something that can be learned by counting the number of questions students get right and wrong on a test. There is something to be gained from looking at which questions received more right answers than wrong ones. Yet for all the value gained by looking at numbers generated by students, we know nothing from such data about the people, the human beings, *homines sapientes*, who are in our classes.

To know something about people, we must enter into relationships with them, and unless a scholar is doing dispassionate research about tyrants, those relationships are based on affection. We must, dare I say it, love our students. Do I enjoy every behavior exhibited by each of my students? I do not. Yet I care about them. I want to know what kinds of music they enjoy, whether they prefer deep dish or hand-tossed pizza, and what they think of the latest blockbuster movie before I spend my money on it. When they return from an illness, I want to know how they are doing and how much longer they will have to be on the crutches. I enjoy listening to their stories of things they learned in another class and the connections they made with ours.

How much of this goes into an artifact that can be displayed in our hallways? None of it does. Which state standard covers such interactions? There is not one. For which portions of the Advanced Placement or

International Baccalaureate exam will these parts of my class prepare my students? There are none that I know of, and if there are any, I frankly do not care. What I care about are the young people...*young* people...with whom I get to share not just life, but some of the most amazing discoveries about life ever made by our fellow human beings across time and space.

Anne Marie was right. It is from such relationships that genuine education, which is the only kind that truly matters, will grow.

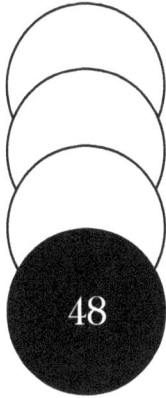

The Shoulders of Education Leadership

A dear friend of mine, Kate Smith, who is an award-winning principal in Australia,[67] uses the expression "shoulder-to-shoulder teaching." She describes going into teachers' classrooms and working with them, teaching alongside them, shoulder-to-shoulder.

Another friend of mine, 2015 Indiana Teacher of the Year Kathy Nimmer,[68] once told me about monthly summits in her district in which she met with central office leaders to share experiences and what she was learning as she traveled our state. It was a time in which all benefited, and she was valued.

And then there was the experience I once had with my post-evaluation conference. The person who evaluated me at that time was my department chair, Traci Rodgers. We quickly moved from talking about the evaluation to discussing the implications of some data I had requested about changes in the demographics of our school and school district. We talked about work our department had some years prior in that area, how our student profile had changed in the intervening years, and what some of the implications could be. And as we talked about numbers, we began to talk about people. We talked about actual students and families. We speculated. We mused. We pondered.

As she left, we acknowledged that we had come up with no solution to any problem and no means of handling any particular challenge. Yet we had done one of the most important things two human beings can do. We had thought together. No, you did misread that last sentence. I did not write that we had taught together, although we were indeed colleagues in the best sense of that word. We had thought together, and that supremely human act can only take place when egos and agendas are set aside and two people walk shoulder-to-shoulder looking in the same direction toward what can be.

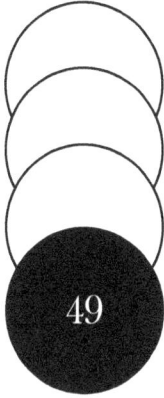

49 I Don't Want an Education

In the classic 1960 film *Spartacus*, the famous gladiator-turned-freedom-fighter played by Kirk Douglas enjoys a rare evening of peace with his beloved Varinia, who was played by Jean Simmons. As they recline in a meadow and indulge in the soft conversation of lovers, their talk turns to knowledge of the wide world.

Spartacus: I know nothing. Nothing! And I want to know. I want to...I want to know.
Varinia: Know what?
Spartacus: Everything. Why a star falls and a bird doesn't. Where the sun goes at night. Why the moon changes shape. I want to know where the wind comes from.

I was at an overnight planning session for the Indiana Junior Classical League at Indiana University, and as I often do when visiting my alma mater, I took a walk around campus during the early morning before our meeting resumed. I followed a path different from my usual course and ended up by Rawles Hall, home of the mathematics department, went in, and found a poster for an upcoming lecture. Apart from definite articles and conjunctions, there was almost no word on that poster that I had either seen before or understood.

As I drifted back past more familiar buildings, I recalled the words of Spartacus and thought as I have so many times about all that I do not know. Like him, I want to know. I want to have a deeper understanding of mathematics so that I can truly grasp the words attributed to Galileo that mathematics is the alphabet with which God wrote the universe.[69] I want to understand the language of numbers and mathematics and how they describe the universe. And with regard to the universe, I want to know how forces work and interact with each other and with matter, forces like the electromagnetic force and gravity and the strong and weak nuclear forces. I want to explore the human sciences and understand the workings of the mind and consciousness and how to know which fonts and colors and arrangements of graphic information are best for reaching certain audiences to communicate certain information, and I want to know how we know such things.

Like most people, I raced through my education. Spelling for fifteen minutes, math for half an hour, followed by reading and lunch and then social studies, P.E., and science. That was a day in elementary school. In junior high and high school, the pace quickened. Every fifty minutes or so a bell rang and you moved down the conveyor belt to the next class. And why? It was mostly to memorize this or that, prove yourself through tests and projects, and then do it again. With such training, how could I have approached undergraduate studies any differently? I remember once during my freshman year at Indiana University sitting in a class thinking I should be back in the dorm room completing some assignment. The absurdity hit me like a thunderclap. Listening to a professor who was an expert in the subject was the reason I was in college, not mindlessly completing homework.

We speak of getting an education, as if it were any other commodity capable of being acquired. I already have too much stuff in my life. I do not need something more. I do not need an education. What I need is to learn. Learning is an inquisitive activity. It is an enterprise of curiosity, mystery, and adventure. It is non-linear and it is not fast. It is not frantic and harried and driven. Learning is deep and therefore slow. As Andrew Marvell mused, had we but world enough and time,[70] I would go back to the university, seek out instructors in matters I wished to learn, and not allow myself to run in a terrified attempt to outpace the inexorable charge of the schooling machine bearing down upon me.

What can teachers do, then, chained as they are inside the belly of the beast and forced to turn the cranks to make it go? We can tantalize our students with tastes of the true, the good, and the beautiful. We can make them thirsty with grains of the curious and mysterious. We can take them to the edge of awe and wonder and inspire them with the possibility of one day being freed from the mechanism of schooling so that they can truly learn.

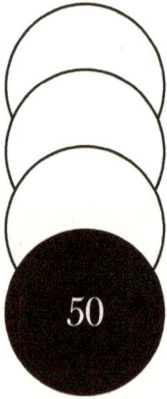

50   Celebrity Teachers

I am not the celebrity hound that my dear friend Marcene is. She has pictures with everyone from Red West of Elvis Presley's "Memphis Mafia" to Dee Snider of Twisted Sister fame. Nevertheless, I was as geeked up as the next guy when my son and I once got to meet Michael Sweet, lead singer and guitarist for the hair-metal band Stryper.

Yet I am a huge, stars-in-the-eyes fan of a certain group of people. It is not sports stars or actors, not politicians or authors; it is teachers.

Some years ago, I attended the National Junior Classical League[71] Convention that was hosted by my own state, Indiana, at my alma mater, Indiana University. While there with over fifteen hundred Latin students, teachers, and professors from around the country for a week of competitions, learning, and fun related to the languages and cultures of ancient Greece and Rome, my wife Melissa, also a Latin teacher, and I had the opportunity to visit with professors from our undergraduate days.

On the first day of the convention, Matt Christ, department chair of Classical Studies at IU, spoke to us before one of the assemblies. As we talked about Classics at the university, I could not help thinking, "I'm talking to the department chair!" A few days later he dined with us at a banquet for all the teachers, and as our talk meandered through Classics at the university and secondary levels, I was again struck by the opportunity I was enjoying.

Mid-week of the convention, I met my good friend Tim Long for breakfast. Tim is a professor emeritus of Classics at IU, and far more than just being my Greek professor, he gave me sage advice on many matters when I was an undergraduate and has remained a good friend whom I often consult whenever Classics-related questions arise. When I left the breakfast table after two hours of conversation, it was as if I had just sat down.

That afternoon Melissa and I had the chance to relive a memory. We sat in Ballantine Hall, where we had so many classes as undergrads, and listened as Ellie Leach presented her work on the mythological paintings in Roman houses. We had been her students in multiple classes, and to have the chance to sit under her instruction again, in the classroom building where it all began for us, was a tremendous thrill.

Then that evening I received an email from Derek Vint. Derek was the office manager and fiscal officer of the Classical Studies department for many years, so we made it a point to visit him the following day, and when I asked how long he had been there, he said that in just another month he would mark forty years. Derek was always the one who assisted us with our class scheduling, and as he gestured to open chairs so we could sit and chat and turned on his window air conditioner for our comfort, we knew we had come home.

Finally, on the last day of the convention, Betty Rose Nagle had us over for pie. Betty Rose taught the first and last classes I took as an undergraduate, the first being on Cicero and the last on Ovid. We have remained friends, and she is often a person I reach out to with my many questions. We spent the morning on her porch, eating wickedly good key lime pie that she had made, and discussing her work with 18th century German-authored Latin texts on human skulls and various other Classics related topics that made me never want to leave. When we did, however, she imparted a box full of books that immediately made their way into my classroom.

The relationship between teachers and students never ends, and like the biggest rock and roll fan, I was giddy with excitement in each of these encounters with friends in education who have had such an effect on my life and what I do. And why should we not be excited to interact with our teachers? They worked with us in our formative years in *loco parentis*, and the places where we learned with them bear the name *alma mater*, nourishing mother. Our teachers and professors are more significant parts of our lives than most celebrities ever will be. The next time you have a chance, pay one of them a visit. It will mean the world to both of you.

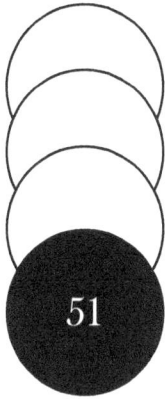

The Human Desire to Know

51

Elisha Ballantine was a professor of mathematics, modern languages, and ancient Greek at Indiana University and was its acting president in 1884. I have countless times passed the plaque that honors him in the building that bears his name on the IU campus, but was struck when I saw it again on one of my visits. He was a professor of mathematics and Greek. In today's age of specialization, this would be an oddity to say the least. A professor of Greek and Latin makes sense, as does a professor of mathematics and computer science. But when was the last time you knew someone who was a professor of mathematics and Greek?

This put me in mind of a former teacher at New Albany High School, my alma mater in New Albany, Indiana. You have no doubt heard of Edwin Hubble and the telescope that bears his name, but did you know that he taught high school physics, mathematics, and Spanish in 1913? He also coached the boys' basketball team.

Men like Ballantine and Hubble reminded me of famed golfer Bobby Jones. In 1922 he earned his B.S. in Mechanical Engineering and in 1924 his

A.B. in English literature. After beginning law school in 1926, and completing only three semesters, he passed the Georgia bar exam and practiced law in Atlanta.

Mathematics and Greek. Spanish and physics. Engineering and literature. There was a time when people pursued a variety of studies. This is not to say that everyone of a bygone era was a polymath, but I do find a certain kinship with those academic souls of yesteryear. The world is vast, history is long, creation is complex, and humans have both discovered and contributed much to the unfolding wonder of it all. When we make education nothing more than training for gainful employment, we miss a great deal. In fact, we miss almost everything. A stick in a forest can help make the fire that keeps me warm through the night, but the forest itself, with its symphony of sounds and the towering columns of its arboreal cathedral that seem to support its stellar dome, is worth beholding in its own right. And while it is true that the quiet contemplation of the evening nature scene now in your head could inspire you toward an act of creativity such as the composition of a poem or a work of painting or photography, there is something more to be gained from the experience. Simply put, it nourishes the soul.

So it is with true education. It may equip students for a task or an occupation. It may provide them with the skills necessary to produce any manner of art, both for service and for art's sake itself. At its core, however, it needs to serve no other purpose than fulfilling the human desire to know. Beware the call of the pragmatic. It is not to be ignored, but it is not the sole purpose of a complete education, which ultimately must be about the soul.

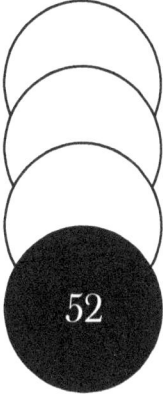

52

Playing With Ideas

The officers of our school's chapter of the Indiana Junior Classical League had arranged a meeting one afternoon, and that should be your first clue that something special was taking place. I did not call the meeting. They did. This extraordinary group of young leaders picked up from their last meeting and began filling my board with dates, ideas, and who would be responsible for accomplishing various tasks. They asked me for help only when needed for such things as emailing a secretary to schedule room use.

I sat back and watched. I listened. And I was astounded as I so frequently am.

After working for a while on recommendations for college-bound seniors, I needed to take a break, so I went next door to the meeting of the Philosophy Club. I sat down next to a retired colleague who continued to sponsor the club she had led for many years when she taught English and Theory of Knowledge. I sat back and watched. I listened. And I was astounded.

A small, diverse group of young people discussed what they could know with regard to science. My colleague did not lead the group. The students led themselves. In fact, one of them had prepared the materials that guided their conversation.

When my children were young, they played with joy and abandon with their toys, and it struck me that what was going on in the Philosophy Club and what was taking place with the officers of the IJCL was the same thing. These young people had outgrown childish objects, but they were playing with the toys appropriate to their age. They were playing with ideas. The philosophy students were trying out their thoughts about the nature of things in public discourse, and they did so as boldly as any child playing in a sandbox. The Latin students gave exercise to their notions of leadership by jumping in and leading.

At play in the field of ideas, these students experienced a uniquely human joy, and it was a pleasure to behold.

53 What Have You Done for Me Lately?

Music fans from the 1980s will remember that the title of this essay is also the title of a Janet Jackson song. That song perfectly captures the disposition of too many students with regard to their own education, and I would suggest that there is something more.

A colleague once pointed out that when students realize that it is mathematically impossible for them to pass, or very unlikely that they will, they often turn to general misbehavior. It is not necessarily anything violent, but with nothing to gain from the class, they create a disruption through talking off topic, playing on their phones, and so forth.

Many will begin pointing fingers at the teachers in whose classes this takes place. They should have been more engaging, these people will say. They should continue finding ways to reach each student to the very last minute of the semester. A student who has gained so little from the class is one more sad example of a system that is failing its students.

Although it is true that a teacher's poor efforts may be the cause of a student's failure to learn, failure to learn itself is no proof of a teacher's poor efforts. Yet what I want to focus on here is the purely consumer mentality at work in students who think that if they gain nothing from the class, then there is no reason for them to be in it, a belief that in their minds justifies their misbehavior.

Each fifty minutes my students and I form a small community. We explore together the language, thought, art, literature, and history of the ancient Roman world. I would, however, be loath to think of my students as parasites, only taking in knowledge and never contributing to the shared journey of discovery that is education. Yes, they are taking something from my class, but they should be contributing something as well, and that contribution is not what they give me in the form of completed assignments and assessments, but the thoughts they speak within the interactions of any given class period. Students have something to contribute by asking questions, both those of simple clarification about a confusing point and those of the genuine curiosity that is the root of the branching nature of learning. They contribute by sharing the connections they make between observations in my class and the reading, learning, and experiences from other parts of their lives. Their contributions take the form of iron sharpening iron as each member of the class makes the others better.

Those entrusted with the development of young minds, teachers, parents, coaches, administrators, teaching assistants, librarians, media specialists, and guidance counselors, along with those less directly yet significantly involved such as policy makers and pundits, must understand that a classroom is not a website where students place their orders and leave with a product. The true classroom, whether or not it is bounded by walls, is a dynamic community of learning, and because it is both dynamic and a community, it requires something of all its members, not merely the teacher. Students who are actively engaged in their learning, even though they may fail to reach a level of achievement that has been desired by someone else, will nevertheless have contributed to the shared journey of discovery and may enjoy the proper confidence that their fellow travelers in class are the better for it.

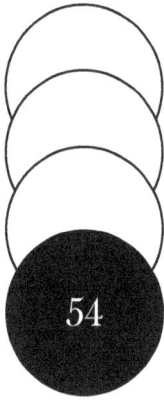

54 A Not Untypical Day in High School

For much of my career, I taught at a public high school of just under 4,000 students. Our classes were huge. We were not elite. And yet the following took place one day. Those who have ears to hear, let them hear.

In my Period 2 class of first-year Latin, one of my students taught the grammar lesson. I had recorded myself teaching key grammar points, posted those videos on our website, and the students were required to watch them at home while taking notes. The following day students would volunteer to teach, or re-present, the lesson. On that day, Samantha not only put the information on the board, but asked questions of her classmates and sought volunteers. She did not merely regurgitate information. She taught.

In my Advanced Placement class, we discussed an alternative form of a verb in Latin poetry. In this instance it was the verb *fulsere*, meaning "they flashed," and one of my students said, "Oh, that's just like in that Catullus poem we read last year where the suns flashed for him." He was referring to Catullus 8, and I simply shook my head in admiring disbelief.

Perhaps it was just that my emotional pump had been primed by discussions over the previous few days. In my third-year Latin class we had read about a murder in 53 B.C. on the Appian Way. The wife of the victim demanded that her husband's corpse be displayed in the forum for all to see, and we discussed the parallel with Emmett Till, whose death in 1955 prompted his mother to have an open casket for her son and for *Jet* magazine to run the pictures. As the story of the ancient murder developed, it described the mob violence that followed and led to the burning of the senate house. My students discussed violence in the modern world and that free speech does not mean shouting "Fire!" in a crowded theater. They discussed the proper limits to freedom that make freedom livable without devolving into chaos.

Just the day before, the Advanced Placement students had discussed the dangerous role of rumor as depicted by the Roman epic poet Vergil and as seen today in our social media. In both the third-year Latin and A.P. discussions, I shared that I was concerned for my students' well-being and that they not find themselves caught up in the kinds of messaging or activities that have led to ruined lives.

And then, after school, a young man who was observing me twice a week from Indiana University in preparation for student teaching, engaged with me in the most heady and delightful of discussions. We talked about his passion for Medieval works. We looked at the prayers of St. Ambrose and talked about St. Augustine, St. Thomas Aquinas, the *Dies Irae*, and the *Stabat Mater*. We talked of Boethius, and he introduced me to 12th century French theologian and poet Alain de Lille.

To be sure, not all days are as rich and satisfying, but those described here are not untypical, and because of that they stand as a testament to both the depth and the breadth it is possible to explore in high school.

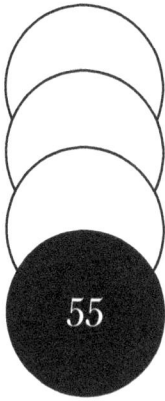

19 + 1 = Unforgettable

One of my best students used his phone in class. I know. We are supposed to embrace technology in education, but I found tears springing to my eyes. This was one of my top students. I have always loved how his mind worked, but for him to use his phone like this. Perhaps I should explain.

It was the Advanced Placement Latin class, and we were reading a section from Book 6 of Vergil's *Aeneid* in English. The students had their Latin texts open, but each one had a different English translation from one of our bookshelves, and they were taking turns reading aloud.

After Katie finished reading Frederick Ahl's 2007 translation of lines 562-586 in which Tisiphone explains to Aeneas what he is looking at in the underworld, Nicholas asked if he could share the 1872 rendering by Christopher Pearse Cranch that he had been following. He was visibly excited, so I encouraged him to do so. At the end of his reading, he talked about how much he loved Cranch's language, even stating that this was the most vivid and creative bit of writing he had read in the past couple of years.

And it was at that point that he took out his phone to photograph the pages, and I nearly cried.

Here was a young man so deeply moved by words that he had to share them. Here, in one of the largest public high schools in Indiana, was a class with students that could share his joy and enthusiasm over the power and beauty of the written word. But did you notice the most important part of this story? It was the *student* who was moved and wanted to savor these words in the community of peers. It was not the teacher forcing him to look at something and demanding, "Don't you think that's wonderful?"

It reminded me of the scene in *Dead Poets Society* in which English teacher Mr. Keating's (Robin Williams) students confront him with his old yearbook and ask what the society was all about.

Student: You mean it was a bunch of guys sitting around reading poetry?

Mr. Keating: No, Mr. Overstreet, it wasn't just "guys." We weren't a Greek organization. We were romantics. We didn't just read poetry, we let it drip from our tongues like honey. Spirits soared, women swooned, and gods were created, gentlemen. Not a bad way to spend an evening, eh?

So, yes, I became emotional when a 19th century translation elicited from one 21st century student a response that was unforgettable for us both.

56 Vivit Lingua Latina

I am about to introduce to you the person who made me so nervous I nearly quit Latin. Since I met my wife in a collegiate Latin class and have taught the language for more than three decades, I am glad I did not, but I was certainly tempted to do so after the first day in Miss Alice Ranck's second-year Latin class at New Albany High School.

When I was a freshman, which in our school district meant the last grade of junior high, I signed up to take German for no higher an academic reason than that this was the language my friends were taking. Because the class was filled, the assistant principal called my parents and said he wanted to enroll me in Latin, for, in his words, he wanted me "to experience Alice Ranck." It would mean walking across the athletic fields to the high school each day, since Latin was not offered at Hazelwood Junior High, but he assured us the effort would be worth it.

As it turned out, my first-year Latin teacher was Joyce Woller, a very nice lady, and I enjoyed the language enough to continue it the following year as a sophomore at the high school. Nothing could have prepared me for that first day. Miss Woller had done a fine job of grounding us in the basics of Latin grammar, but what neither she nor anyone else could have prepared us to handle was the force of nature that was Miss Ranck. She talked so fast! It was like taking a sip from a fire hose! I thought I would never be able to keep up, and when I told my parents, they asked if I thought I should drop the class. I decided to stay with it, and my life has never been the same.

Miss Ranck had a white bumper sticker on her chalkboard from the American Classical League[72] that read in purple letters, *Vivit Lingua Latina*, and indeed the Latin language continued to live through her instruction. There was, of course, the grammatical instruction, which, after decades of my own teaching, I can testify was as sound as could be. Much of my own instruction, from style to curriculum arrangement, stems from her. There was also the historical and the mythological material, and again I find phrases about Caesar and Cicero echoing from her classroom in my own.

Then there was the fun. We had an annual Roman banquet, complete with Roman dress and high school students reclining on their elbows in the school gym to eat Roman food. There was Latin Club, with its "pound party" fundraisers in which students brought in a pound of food for auction. And there was *certamen*. This is an academic competition that sees students playing in teams to answer questions about the language, history, and culture of Greco-Roman antiquity. Miss Ranck took us to play *certamen* (pronounced *care-TAH-mun*) in far off Muncie and Terre Haute, and my mom often drove, following her little, blue Volkswagen Rabbit in the wee, dark hours of a Hoosier Saturday morning.

To be fair, this is all a nice description of a good teacher, perhaps even one above average, but it does not explain why this woman from Fountain City, Indiana, should have become a legend. It does not give a hint why she was named 1982-1983 Secondary Teacher of the Year by the Classical Association of the Middle West and South.[73] It does not explain why she was the 1985 Teacher of the Year for the New Albany-Floyd County Community School Corporation and a candidate for Indiana Teacher of the Year. It does not give even the slightest clue why hundreds of her former students have joined an online group in her honor, have traveled over the years to visit her, and have shared with her weddings, births, and graduations that they have celebrated. Perhaps those students took to heart the wisdom of

Miss Ranck's favorite Roman author Cicero, who in his essay on friendship, wrote, "*Qui esset tantus fructus in prosperis rebus, nisi haberes qui illis aeque ac tu ipse gauderet?*" (De Amicitia, 22) "How great would be the enjoyment in good times if you did not have someone who would rejoice in them as much as you?"

Here at last we come to the heart of what made Miss Ranck a beloved figure in the lives of her students. It is simply that, heart. When she was inducted into the New Albany High School Hall of Fame in 2008, she said in her acceptance remarks, "It is our responsibility as educators to provide a sound education based on ethical principles. Innate within every human being is first the desire to be noticed and to be loved, then comes the need to be taught to learn how to learn. It is the role of the teacher to notice and yes, to love the student so much that he is ready to learn, and in turn develop all of his potential. What better way for a teen-ager to learn to live honorably and well than to read from the literary masterpieces of Cicero."

Miss Ranck noticed her students. Whether they were in her Latin class or not, all the children at New Albany High School were her students, and she greeted them warmly each day. Those who had the good fortune to be her students were blessed by her demanding love, a love that would not tolerate anything less than a student's best. And when, in the course of human nature, a student came ill-prepared to class, that student heard the familiar refrain, "Preparation will cure what ails you!"

She inspired at least three of her students to become Latin teachers, and all of us have had long careers. From middle school to high school to undergraduate levels of Latin and Classics, I estimate that I have taught around three thousand students. During that time I have supervised eleven student teachers, nine of whom went on to teach Latin. Now consider that Miss Ranck's other two students who became Latin teachers had similar careers. Do you see where this is going? Add on others of her students who entered the teaching field, albeit not in Latin, and took her wisdom and caring to their students. Add to that the rest of her students whose lives were enriched by their time with her and who were better employees, neighbors, husbands, wives, and parents because they entered the grand conversation with the greatest ancient authors, a conversation hosted by one who modeled what she taught. Ask them. They will tell you that this encomium is based in fact, not hyperbole, and you will come to see what truly makes a legend.

One of the happiest days of my high school life was Tuesday, April 29th, 1986. Miss Ranck had loaned me one of her copies of *New Latin Grammar* by Charles Bennett, and in it I discovered something about the imperative plural of deponent verbs, those tricky words that have only passive forms and only active meanings. I shared it with her, and she did something that made my day. She gave me that copy of Bennett's Grammar and inscribed in the front a message that ended, "May the best of everything be yours in the future, Steve! You've already earned it." I can still remember walking to my next class without my feet touching the ground.

Miss Ranck more than earned the respect of the students, parents, and colleagues with whom she worked. The Romans believed that a person's *fama*, that which was said about someone, was the most important thing, for it would live even after that person had passed from this life to the next. If *fama* has that sort of lasting power, then Miss Ranck's must surely shine beyond that of most. In fact, as Vergil wrote of Jupiter's intention for the Roman people in the first book of his *Aeneid*, so it is with the *fama*, the legend, of Miss Ranck, or as many of her students called her, Miss Alice, even after she retired to marry her high school sweetheart and became Mrs. Alice Hettle. It has *nec metas, nec tempora*, neither limits nor duration, and through the lives of her many students will stand *sine fine*, without limit. Because this is true, we can all borrow words from Catullus in poem 101, "*atque in perpetuum, Magistra, ave atque vale.*" "And into eternity, O Teacher, hail and farewell."

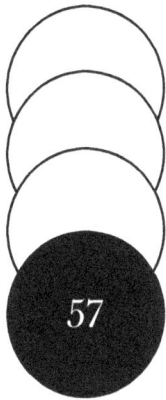

57 Entering a Story

While visiting the Grand Tetons and Yellowstone one summer, we saw a young tyke wearing a Batman costume. Most people give little thought to children dressing up as superheroes. It is common for young ones to pretend to be their favorite characters from books and movies or people who seem larger than life like firefighters and astronauts, yet I would suggest this is not the province of children alone. Adults, too, enjoy entering into larger stories.

I am a huge fan of the Longmire novels by Craig Johnson,[74] so when we prepared for our trip to the West, I packed one of them. It has always taken me more time and been more a delight to pick out which books to pack for a trip than which clothes to put into my suitcase. I had been re-reading the Longmire series in order and was in the middle of *Any Other Name*, so that went into my bag along with a few other books.

Craig Johnson is an award-winning author who is featured in Buffalo Bill Center of the West[75] in Cody, Wyoming. He crafts stories that invite readers into another world and make them long to revisit once the last page has been turned. His characters are carefully and exquisitely crafted, and the settings he describes rightfully hold a place as participants every bit as vivid as the human players. How, then, does one whose inner child has not been lost enter into such tales?

For starters, I wanted to read one of those novels while in the places near where they are set. I read while we stayed in Driggs and Island Park, Idaho, and in the Wyoming cities of Cheyenne and Cody. In the liner notes to John Cougar Mellencamp's 1985 album *Scarecrow*, we find this. "The highway between John's house and the studio where these songs were recorded cuts through a stretch of Indiana where the land is fertile and full of growth. It is from this land and its people that these songs are born, and though it is not necessary to know this to enjoy and appreciate them, it does lend a certain understanding for those who care to think about such things." Serious readers care to think about such things, and it was one way for me to enter into the stories that Craig has created by reading them in the West. But wait, as the infomercials say. There is more.

The Busy Bee Café often provides nourishment for protagonist Sheriff Walt Longmire, and though in the books it sits in the fictitious town of Durant, Wyoming, in reality it exists in Buffalo, where we made a stop just to take a picture. We would have eaten there, but the Bee is closed on Sundays. Had it been open, I would have ordered Walt's usual, but to find out what that is you will need to read the books.

Yet the picture I was most excited to take was with the road sign for Ucross, Wyoming, population 25. That is the home of author Craig Johnson, a fact that he proudly notes on the inside flap of each book jacket.

Before you start thinking this is all a bit much, I will have you know that it is no exaggeration that thousands of people liked the pictures I posted in the various online Longmire fan groups. I would also point out that you probably own some apparel dedicated to your favorite sports figures or musicians, and this leads us back to my original point. We like to enter into other stories. It is part of human nature. Why do you think Homer's *Iliad* has been so popular for nearly three thousand years? We thrill to the adventures of Achilles and Hector and if only for a short time are transported to places we can only imagine, gaining new perspectives on life as we go.

Thus ends the literary portion of this essay, and thus begins the educational. Teachers have an opportunity as no one else does to help young people enter into other stories. In fact, although it may not be written in their job description, it is one of the most important things they do. From kindergarten through twelfth grade, a child's understanding is quite limited. Children simply have not lived much life, yet they can grow far beyond the constraints of time and space through entering into the grand stories of history, science, literature, and the arts. Their teachers, however, must be guides who have not lost their own love of entering into stories. A dry, crabbed person is not a fit companion for adventure.

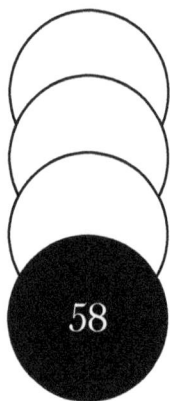

58 Too Fast

It has been a long time since I was in kindergarten, putting a big, red F on a quiz I had made for my grandmother. Back then, I thought that was what teaching was all about, but then I grew up. Now, grading is one of my least favorite parts of my job as a teacher, as it is for many if not most teachers. I do not enjoy the tedium of it, but there is another reason grading is a particular challenge for me. It takes too long. Now, you may be thinking, "Just assign less work, or create assignments that are easier to grade." That solution, however, misses the root cause of my problem. Grading takes a long time for me because I am too fast.

In the 1964 film *Becket*, an adaptation of the 1959 Jean Anouillh play *Becket or the Honour of God*, King Henry II (Peter O'Toole) falls out with his onetime friend Thomas Becket (Richard Burton), whom he had helped make the Archbishop of Canterbury. In one of the most famous, although undoubtedly not the first, instances of plausible deniability, Henry muses among his noblemen, "Will no one rid me of this meddlesome priest?" The nobles take this as a command from their sovereign and head out to murder Becket in the cathedral. Yet it is what Henry says immediately after his provocative query that has always struck me as the heart of this story. "Are all around me cowards, like myself? Are there no men left in England?" He then clutches his chest and gasps, "It's my heart. It's too fast. Too fast." This is not a reference to an irregular heartbeat, but makes use of an older definition of "fast" meaning steadfast or deeply fixed.

Henry is torn between his need to establish his authority and his steadfast feeling of friendship with Becket. In his words, his heart is too fast. What on earth could be the comparison between this sort of anguish and the challenge to a teacher grading an assignment? It is just this. Like Henry, I am torn by the need to do something, namely, to assign a grade, and the deeply fixed feelings of admiration and inspiration that threaten to overwhelm me as I read what students have written. My heart is too fast.

At some point each year, my third-year Latin students read selections from the writings of the Stoic philosopher Seneca, and upon completion they must take their reading a step further. Seneca had written his philosophy in the form of letters to a friend, and these students must write a philosophical epistle of their own. Additionally, they must consider which of Seneca's epistles meant the most to them, which one caused them to look at something in a new way or even for the first time, and which contained ideas they were likely to apply in their own lives. Everything that follows was student authored. Take the time to read what they wrote, even the longer passages, and as you do, pause to admire the thoughts of which teenaged students are capable.

Philosophia Mea

The following are excerpts from what these students wrote, in imitation of Seneca, in the form of a philosophical epistle.

"A lot of times you go through life thinking you need someone's permission to do something so simple. You might think you need permission from yourself. You probably think that you need to have your life all sorted out or have everything marked off your to-do list before you do something you want. But go ahead and give yourself the grace to enjoy life a little bit."

"To My Dearest (Future!) Daughter,

Being a girl isn't easy. Women are so quick to judge other women, just based on what they see externally. I want you to know that you are perfect just the way you are. The only opinion about you that matters is your own. There will be times where you doubt yourself, where you lack self-confidence, where you may have a poor body-image, or where you make mistakes. But these adversities are all just a part of life that everyone faces at least once. I myself have struggled with all of these. My sweet daughter, always remember that "You are braver than you believe, stronger than you seem, and smarter than you think." Just being you is more than enough, and I will always love and be proud of you!

With Endless Love,

Mom"

"Do not live an outward life. I urge you, my friend, to build a life that can be self-contained. Do not depend on other people or things, which pass or change with time, but create a place within your soul where you may retreat to find peace and contentment. I do not say that you must withdraw from the world; on the contrary, you must find joy in as many things as possible. Suffering, it seems, waits for us everywhere. Indeed, it is impossible to live a fully joyful life; there is no one, I tell you, who can be joyful in every moment, but you must strive to do so. The man who ceases in his walking to listen more closely to a bird or look more closely at a flower is a man who lives a full life. You must be predisposed to contentment. The man who relies on other people or remarkable events for his daily happiness is like the man who walks out to an island at low tide and does not know how to swim. He is at the mercy of the tides and can never be certain of his safety or free to travel where he wishes. Therefore, dearest friend, carry your joy with you everywhere you go, and do not leave it at the mercy of the world."

"Be wary of jealousy. To combat this you must strive for the virtue of gratitude. But how do you do this? Aristotle taught virtue is the mean between two vices, so gratitude is the mean between jealousy, which is wanting someone's good thing or fortune for your own, and anhedonia, not wanting good for yourself. A great way to counter jealousy is to break yourself of your attachments to possessions since they will never truly bring you happiness; human relationship brings true happiness."

"I advise you not to allow life's potential stresses to tear you down. Parcel the tasks so you can better manage them, and you will find that they truly weren't as stressful as you thought them to be. If you claim not to have time for breaks, know that you are responsible for your own time management, and you should not allow others to take your time away with things that will not allow you to grow your mind."

The Most Meaningful of Seneca's Epistles

Epistle 20 was especially interesting. One particularly meaningful sentence was, "I advise you this: that you not be miserable before the time, since those things at which you paled in fear (as if about to happen), perhaps may never come, for they certainly have not come yet." This was extremely eye-opening, since I often will stress about things that are completely out of my control. Worrying is just making my life harder and causing me extra harm.

I found epistle thirty-eight very meaningful since in it, Seneca states to use effective words rather than many words. I found this statement inspiring since I am a pretty introverted person and sometimes get annoyed with myself or others get annoyed with me for not talking a lot when in a social setting. I think it is very important to state that which has value and meaning rather than just a bunch of meaningless words.

I found epistle eighty-eight very meaningful due to Seneca's emphasis on the idea that titles and degrees and other things which are considered "important" in our modern society are not really that important. What is important is that you are a good person. I found this epistle especially touching since I am not really wanting to go to college and so many people have told me that I am ruining my life by doing that and am not being smart.

Epistle LII was meaningful to me because, as a teenager, I try to look for someone to be an example. It can be discouraging when it seems like you can't find anyone, but this epistle reminded me that my options aren't limited to those that I know personally. Ones that came before me can be examples too.

Epistle 38 was meaningful to me because I find myself rambling a lot and many of the words I say are unnecessary. Seneca says to use fewer words with greater meaning and this is something I need to work on.

Which Epistle Prompted You To Consider Something New?

In Epistle 44, Seneca talks about how philosophy is above no one. This is an idea that I have never thought about before. I have always been intimidated by the idea of philosophical thinking, because I work better in more black-and-white ways of thinking. I enjoyed the part where Seneca said that philosophy did not receive Plato as a noble man, but Plato was made noble through philosophy.

The idea in epistle 2 about retaining something from what you read to protect [against] the plagues of life is a new concept to me. I have always known that reading is supposed to teach you a lesson that you can use in your life, but I had never thought about it as building a defense against plagues of evil. This concept makes me want to read more so that I can have the best defenses possible.

I believe that Seneca's thoughts on teaching and learning helped me to see those things in a new light. Seneca talks about really digesting material and truly understanding it as well as focusing on the actual useful and practical things that can help me to be a better person as well as bettering others.

The idea that made me think in a different way was the idea that you lose credibility if you are not willing to act on your words. I am now going to think my words through and try to back them up with my actions.

Which Piece of Seneca's Advice Might You Apply in Your Life?

The idea that time is the one thing that we are truly in control of is one thing that was discussed in Epistle 1. He talked about how time is extremely "slippery," as well as how easy it is for us to let other people take our valuable time away from us. Personally, I have always prided myself on being decent at time management with my school work; however, I have always put that above everything else in my life. While this has benefited me from an academic standpoint, life is more than school.

One idea I would likely put into practice is the idea discussed in epistle XXVIII, where Seneca suggests that a person should not change their 'climate,' but they should change their spirit. An example of this is that sometimes I do not want to do my homework. Even though I know I must do it in order to get good grades, I sometimes feel like giving up on it. However, instead of thinking about how boring the homework itself is, I like to think about how I will feel once I am done and have gotten a good grade. This is an example of a person changing their spirit.

One idea that I would put into practice is the idea, in letter seventy-six, of always learning. Seneca says that learning must go on as long as you do not know something or as long as you live. I think this one is important to practice in my life because people need to keep learning and growing as much as they can.

An idea I am most likely to put into practice is from epistle 71. In this epistle Seneca states that you must plan for your whole life rather than just parts of your life. We must think more of the end goal rather than just one step at a time. I think about where I am considering going to college. I must also consider what I will do after college and where it will take me.

What career will I choose? I must think more of the future rather than just tomorrow.

I would put into practice the ideas of epistle 33. I have consistently memorized content for tests throughout middle and high school, and forgot all that information directly after it was over. Sometimes, I don't even know or understand the content; rather, I memorize the facts for rehearsal on the test. I need to start fully understanding the content and truly putting it in memory before I have the ability to rehearse it.

59 Sharing a Classroom

I teach in a classroom with many, many other teachers. In fact, I have never taught alone but have always been engaged in a most collaborative enterprise, for I have had the pleasure of working alongside some of the greatest teachers the world has ever known.

There are Socrates and Plato and Alexander Pope, to say nothing of Catullus, Cicero, Horace, Ovid, and Vergil. The history teachers have their say thanks to Livy and Tacitus, and of course, Homer holds a mighty sway.

Sometimes they speak their native Greek or Latin, and sometimes they speak in English, but always they are there, guiding the conversations I have with my students. Even when their voices cannot be heard directly, they are teaching nonetheless, for they are like the waters described by William Butler Yeats in "The Lake Isle of Innisfree."

I will arise and go now, for always night and day
I hear lake water lapping with low sounds by the shore;

While I stand on the roadway, or on the pavements grey,
I hear it in the deep heart's core.

Although the majority of my fellow teachers speak their wisdom from across the centuries, there are more modern educators as well, speaking from my bookshelves to matters of linguistics and philosophy and the natural sciences.

Surely, you say, these do not all make their way into the daily curriculum of a high school Latin class. Surely it would not be appropriate for them to do so. Isn't a secondary language class about nouns and verbs and learning the basics? No, they do not all make their way into our daily lessons, at least not explicitly so, but I disagree with the notion that any of these teachers should not be allowed through the door. In 1970, G. P. Goold, who over his illustrious career served as the chair of Classics departments at Harvard, University College London, and Yale, as well as serving as the chief editor of the Loeb Classical Library for twenty-five years, wrote a most unfortunate statement with which I took issue in an article I wrote a few years ago about a textual difficulty in Vergil's *Aeneid*. Goold wrote, "An elementary teacher, to reach in due season the end of his curriculum, must every hour turn a Nelson eye to serious problems and refrain from pursuing truth beyond the charted boundaries of the textbook." I wrote in response, "I would argue that the true *magister* can never be so bound, but must, along with the students, pursue the truth, no matter how anfractuous the path."[76]

And if truth, rather than the important but necessarily lesser goals of skills proficiency and career readiness, is the foundation and *raison d'être* of education, then surely there must be another teacher in my classroom, even the one who claimed to be truth itself, Jesus Christ.[77]

You see, all of these great teachers have taught me. I am the product of their wisdom, eloquence, and art, and in that way alone, they are teaching my students as surely as I am. Because I have spent considerable time with many of them, their words and ideas are also at the ready when I attempt to do what all teachers do, make connections. Education is essentially helping someone see that this is that. In its simplest expression it may be an equation, for example one connecting the ideas of 2 + 2 and 4. In more complex forms it can be seen in metaphors, allusions, and parables. Indeed, the metaphoric nature of all language points to the this-is-that nature of communication, of which formal education is but one particular instance. For this reason, the assassination of President Kennedy can make its way into a reading of Caesar in Gaul. The dual nature of light as wave and particle will enter into a discussion about the opening of Vergil's *Aeneid*. Even Disney's *The Lion King* will help to illustrate the aspects of Catiline's conspiracy and the fertile ground for demagoguery among the poor and disenfranchised.

Just as these secular teachers weave their way seamlessly and effortlessly through our exploration of Latin, so I am blessed now, somewhere past the midpoint of my career, to teach in a school where we are free to offer a complete approach to learning, one that does not exclude faith as a way of knowing. My students and I can easily make references to Scripture just as we do to writings by Plato or Homer. Although it is my name on the door, my classroom is actually crowded with the greatest of all teachers, and I am more than grateful to share with them the delightful, exciting, and provocative calling of teaching.

Philosophy and Education

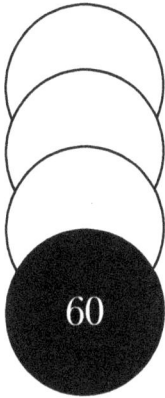

Without Classification in the Pigeonhole Age

Ours is the age of the specialist, and long gone is the day of the educated amateur, the person of letters who could paint, write, and serve in elected office, who could lead in battle and yet publish in science and compose sonnets. The vapid dating line, "What's your sign?" has given way to the even more insulting, because it is so limiting, "What's your major?"

For this and other reasons, Samuel Rocha's *A Primer for Philosophy & Education*[78] will be a challenging read in the current age. It does not fit nicely within the pigeonhole of an accepted educational theory. It does not even fit in that most elite and revered of pigeonholes, the one that says we should break free from pigeon holes. Instead, it weaves its way through a variety of thoughts, poetically meditating on a concept so rich and deep that some may mistake it for something trite and commonplace. Often a pearl of great price is hidden in an ordinary field.

This comes as no surprise after Rocha's acknowledgment in the preface of his debt to William James. He observes that James "didn't always write to or for an exclusive field of peers, due in large measure to the fact that he never belonged to a single field in the first place – he began in anatomy and physiology, moved to psychology, and ended in philosophy with major interests in religion and metaphysics. Perhaps a better way to think about him is this: James belonged to a field of study coincidentally, classified by whatever he was working on at the moment, but never limited by or to that classification."[79]

This is what the world needs and in fact has always needed. Fortunately, there do seem to be a few in any given age capable of answering this need. These are the broadly learned, those driven not by the party line, but by insatiable curiosity and interest in the mysteries of creation. They are the deep readers who will move from Alexander Pope's epitaph for Isaac Newton to Newton's scientific writings. They engage meaningfully in casual conversations on everything from politics to art to literature to theology to sports to finances, with reference not just to unconsidered opinion, but to carefully considered articles and books.

Such a person is not interested in jargon for an academic elite. Such a person is interested most in that shared journey of discovery taken with interlocutors, friends, and students. Rocha notes of James that he "published mostly works of popular philosophy that began as lectures he presented to audiences of all kinds of people. He also frequently wrote essays, reviews, and letters to periodicals and popular journals.... [H]e had a deep sensitivity to what I call 'pastoral philosophy' – an ordinary sense of philosophy that is thoroughly and principally educational."[80]

St. Augustine wrote some of the greatest works of Christian theology while engaged in the work of a bishop. Indeed, it was in response to pressing issues of his day that had practical relevance for his flock that he did his thinking and writing. In his 1984 speech "Advice to Christian Philosophers,"[81] which has since become a seminal text, Alvin Plantinga proposed that Christian philosophers need not be bound by the limits of what their non-Christian peers set for philosophical discussion. Their work, inasmuch as it is conducted in and for the particular community of those confessing Christ, has a duty to respond to the matters most relevant to that community.

Clearly standing in such a tradition, Rocha has written his slender book with a particular audience in mind, his students. It is first and foremost a love letter, a paternal (yet never paternalistic) love letter from a paidagogos to his pupils. Because, like James, Rocha will not be limited to a particular classification and because his approach is one of "pastoral philosophy," fully appreciating what he has to say will require the setting aside of pet classifications. Having made it through to the end of his book, I can assure you that it will be worth the effort to do so.

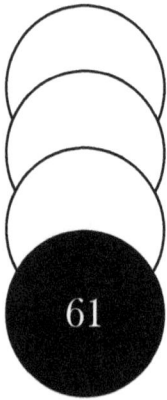

61 Mastering the Craft

There is a sense in the popular imagination that if it is a science, then anyone can do it. If it is an art or a craft, then it is something only for those so gifted. This is not entirely a bad way to look at things. Broadly taken, science is about breaking things down and understanding how their components work, and this understanding applies fairly well from everything like baking a cake to repairing a car engine to launching a rocket into space. If you lay out the steps along with a parts or ingredients list, you should be able to do the thing.

Of course, we know that even in a scientific endeavor, some are simply better at it than others. When it comes to the truly creative side of the equation, the side that deals with intuitive leaps and connections, few of us are Einsteins. Even Einstein acknowledged that there is a beauty to certain equations, so there is unquestionably an artistic aspect to science. Similarly, the science of breaking something down so others can do it can be applied in the graphic arts. Many of us remember the paint-by-numbers books we enjoyed as children.

When it comes to education, the current trend has unquestionably been to see it as a science. We measure and track growth and use data to make many, if not most, of our decisions. Workshops present tips and tricks of the trade so that teachers may replicate in their classrooms what others have accomplished. There is some need for this. There is a greater need for teachers than can be supplied by the Michelangelos of pedagogy. We simply must have some people who are trained to draw Tippy the Turtle.

That, however, is not what Sam Rocha's book *A Primer for Philosophy & Education* is about. As he clearly states, "[T]he craft of philosophy and education is what we are after."[81] In other words, he is after the art, not the science. Because that is what he seeks, he continues, "If the labor and artistry of these intertwined crafts does not interest you, then you should certainly not begin. Disinterest breeds a lack of seriousness. Quit for now and go discover something about which you can be serious. Go paint a house or run a marathon. Learn and master a different, but equally worthwhile craft."[82]

This is not harsh, but helpful. Education is not for those who are uninspired to master the hard work of their craft. Yes, even masters must train, as Michelangelo did under Ghirlandaio. There are many reasons to enter the field of education, but not all of them are worthwhile. Some simply enjoy a subject matter and can think of nothing else to do with a major in it. Some like to be around children. There are those who teach until something better comes along. The increasingly popular balanced calendar has likely weeded out those who wanted a job with three months off in the summer. Whatever a person's reason for pursuing the craft of education, if it is insufficient to motivate and inspire the necessary work, then it is a poor reason.

Now, this is not so arrogant and high-minded as it may sound. It is not saying, "If you are found unworthy of us elites, then go forth and do something lesser with your inferior life." There are many worthwhile crafts. Be a doctor, a pastor, an attorney. Pursue business or politics or sports.

This is also not saying that you must be a Michelangelo. The Tippy-the-Turtle-drawers can be just as committed to mastering their craft. They may not have the flight of fancy or the stroke of genius that befalls the born artist, but they can be just as diligent in doing the work to develop what talents they do have. What matters is being inspired and interested enough to do so.

Education - The Wild and Vast Frontier

The 2002 animated film *Spirit: Stallion of the Cimarron* did not win best animated film, but it should have. It tells the story of a mustang who cannot and will not be tamed. As Roger Ebert rightly observed in his review,[83] the film lacks cutesy animal characters and silly misadventures and therefore is able to tell a compelling tale. Even adults leaving this film will feel a slight pang as they return to their carefully ordered world, wondering in the depths of their hearts what it would be like to be truly free.

Education has more to do with the wild mustang than the gelding, despite systems that have done everything from whacking students with rulers to moving them along on a conveyor belt every fifty minutes. If that is a shocking notion, then be prepared for even more arresting prose poetry from Samuel Rocha in his book *A Primer for Philosophy & Education.*

"Education cannot be institutionalized or corralled. Beautiful teaching requires an explicit, philosophical interest in education – in the widest sense. A gifted teacher always sees more to things than the institution or the profession dictates. Any teacher worthy of the name sees the *person.*

[E]ducation cannot be domesticated. [I]t is so wild and vast."[84]

This is something unlikely to be appreciated on a typical teacher evaluation. There simply is not room for such vision in the spreadsheet columns that track student growth on standardized assessments. Yet if we can risk the danger of attending to that pang in our hearts, we will know in a way that cannot be measured that Rocha is right.

The reason true education is vast and wild and incapable of being corralled, which is to say tied down, measured, and mandated, is that it is about people. As Rocha observed, the true teacher sees the person.

I made the mistake early in my career of seeing the curriculum first. A veteran teacher assigned to mentor me at my first school met with me to discuss opening week activities. I wanted to talk about how to approach teaching Latin grammar to eighth graders, but she wanted to talk about establishing the classroom environment. In the brash omniscience of a newly minted undergraduate, I was sure I knew more. I was wrong, and I discovered that, fortunately, rather quickly.

Because education is a human enterprise of humans leading humans on the journey of discovery, it is not a cut and dried affair. It requires a great deal of work of an abstract nature, certain mental gymnastics, if you will, but for now, consider this. Would you be willing to do the work necessary to become a true teacher if it meant knowing the wild, untamed freedom of true education?

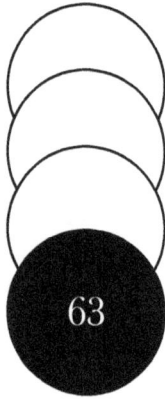

63   **Tools of the Trade**

In *A Primer for Philosophy & Education*, Samuel Rocha links two fields of human endeavor that may, to the contemporary mind, have little to do with each other. We all know what education is, right? But isn't philosophy something for the uber-nerdy? Don't you have to be some kind of Plato to engage in philosophy?

As its Greek etymology shows, philosophy is nothing more, and nothing less, than the love of wisdom. Because of this, Rocha encourages us that "Erudition is not necessary for original philosophy. [Y]ou will not need encyclopedic stores of authors and titles of books you most likely haven't read. You will need only a clear, curious mind and a heart that is passionate and wild enough to sustain and feed a lively, probing imagination."[85]

Thinking philosophically is the heart of the work required to master the craft of education. You do not need any tools beyond what Rocha has laid out, but allow me to offer a few additional words of advice.

Nurture your own childlike sense of wonder. I have been engaged in the study of Latin and Classical Studies for more than thirty years, but I continue to be amazed at a turn of phrase in Ovid or Vergil. My students ask questions that I have never considered, and suddenly I want to know, too. A text I have read countless times takes on a new meaning and relevance because I am reading it on *this day* with *this group* of people as opposed to yesterday with someone else. Rocha observes, "The ordinary, when attended to closely and with care, is extraordinary all on its own – and we are educated by it."[86]

Ask provocative questions of your colleagues. Ask them off-the-wall things. Do not merely start discussions, but rather provoke them. See what happens. I have been blessed to enjoy some of the most thoughtful colleagues over the years. I have had scintillating conversations during passing periods, at the copy machine, and in the hall after school with colleagues in the Social Studies, English, Science, Math, P.E., Art, and Performing Arts departments.

Do not let the details get you down. I was a good student growing up, and getting my homework done was just a part of who I was. I had a revelatory moment, though, as a freshman at Indiana University. I was sitting in Prof. Betty Rose Nagle's class on Cicero and thinking, "I wish this class would end so I could get back to my room and work on an assignment for this class." The absurdity hit me with a flash. The assignment was meant to complement the class. The class was the thing, not the assignment. I was letting the details get in the way. Your grading will get done. Copies will get made for the quiz. If there is a good, deep, philosophical discussion going on, jump in with both feet. This is part of the work you must do to develop your craft.

At the end of the day, ask what it is your students really need from you. Anyone can make cutouts and handouts and online presentations. What do they need that only you can offer? You must discover this, and it can only be done through philosophical reflection and exploration, which, fortunately, is open to anyone with a curious mind, a passionate heart, and a probing imagination.

64   This is That

Years ago I had the opportunity of taking Douglas Hofstadter to dinner before he gave the inaugural lecture in an annual series a colleague and I had developed at our high school. This Pulitzer-winning author who works in cognitive science, philosophy, computer science, and seemingly everything else, spoke on what may have seemed a strange topic for him. His talk was titled "Is Modern Poetry Complete Rubbish," and in it he took issue with poets who write in such confused ways and on such esoteric topics that no one reads their work. In fact, he found the poetry of the song "Surrey with a Fringe on Top" from the musical *Oklahoma!* to be of greater value than much contemporary work, which he considered little more than prose with a ragged right margin. Even in discussing other, more heady topics, he had a particular abhorrence for jargon. In that he reminded me of the character Margrethe Bohr, who in Daniel Frayn's play *Copenhagen* persistently asked her husband, Niels, and Werner Heisenberg to put their theories in plain language.

Samuel Rocha knows that plain-language explanations are at the heart of good education and good philosophy. In *A Primer for Philosophy & Education*, he writes, "Description is on grand display in the art of kindergarten teaching. A great kindergarten teacher can describe things to young children in simple, vivid, lively, and clear – but perfectly ordinary – ways. If philosophers could be half as descriptive as an excellent kindergarten teacher, they would become far better philosophers. At the very least, people might understand them better."[87]

To be sure, there are times when a fifty-cent word is simply the best word for the job, and no dime store variant will do. Wordsmiths also like tossing around certain words because they are fun to say or we just like the ring of them. I remember getting quite excited about the words "anfractuous" and "penthemimeral caesura" that I needed to use in an article I was writing, and it is likely I included them here because I still take a nerdy glee in them. The bottom line, though, is that we like jargon because it makes us sound intelligent, which is perfectly understandable, but not really well suited to education. Unfortunately, because the profession of education has often been held in little esteem, and the situation is only more grave today, those involved in it look to anything to raise the esteem of their profession and themselves. This often leads us to the embrace of jargon, and even in our attempts to be clear, we more often than not end up trying to eschew obfuscation rather than just getting rid of confusion.

Yet we must remember what we are about, and Rocha points the way. "This is what philosophy and education set out to do: to show things as they are, as best they can. No more and no less."[88] Put another way, ours is the business of saying, "This is that."

Such work forms the core of what I do as a Latin teacher. We 21st century English speakers are studying in the United States an inflected language and its literature from a culture over two millennia and half a world away. When we try to understand why different noun declensions produce different forms for the same cases, I bring out the analogy of auto manufacturers. Chevy, Ford, and Dodge all make cars, trucks, and minivans. All cars do the same basic things, all trucks have the same basic features, and all minivans are essentially the same, but they look different depending on the company that made them. In the same way, a direct object from one Latin declension ends with *-am*, but one from another declension ends with *-um*. They are both direct objects, but they look different. This is that. The same kind of explanation goes on through all our years of study, whether I am comparing a scene from Caesar's war exploits with the movie *Boyz 'n' the Hood* or the rights of the Catilinarian conspirators with Americans caught in acts of treason. This is that.

I still enjoy the good, nerdy, fifty-cent word, but I tend to enjoy it more by myself or with certain colleagues and friends. When it comes to teaching, I am always looking for a simpler and clearer way of saying something. This is not dumbing anything down. It is communicating. As students and their culture change, this can be an ever-shifting endeavor. Indeed, Rocha observes, "This restless philosophical and educational project is always a work of art, striving for harmony, attunement, and balance."[89] Then again, such striving is part of the great enjoyment of it all. As poet and professor Timothy Steele titled one of his books, "*All the Fun's in How You Say a Thing.*"

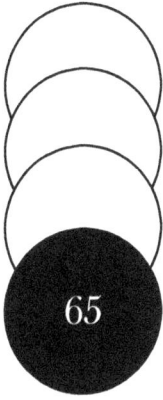

Nothing More Than Happy Accidents

65

"First, let's be clear about what philosophy and education do *not* amount to, what they do *not* offer in return: philosophy and education do not amount to grades, diplomas, or the byproducts of schooling."

If that sentence does not make you slam on the brakes and realize how subversive Samuel Rocha's book *A Primer for Philosophy & Education* is, I do not know what will. Ask anybody. Students will tell you education is precisely about grades and diplomas. Parents and legislators will say that it is all about the byproduct, namely, a job.

Rocha not only takes aim at this ultra-pragmatic view, but observes that it is pervasive throughout our educational system. "In many colleges and universities, there are students who care more about being on the list of some person they hardly know (the Dean), based on three numbers and a decimal point (their grade point average), than they do about anything else related to their studies. Sadly, these people have been conditioned to feel and act this way in previous schooling institutions and elsewhere, too. There has never been an infant who cared about grades, awards, or credentials."[90]

In this Rocha takes us back to Plato's cave and the poor prisoners who award prizes for correctly guessing at shadows. One of the most challenging classes I have had the pleasure to teach is Theory of Knowledge, a course required for the International Baccalaureate diploma. Students in the IB program are at the top of their academic game, but when they take TOK, they often get jarred from their routine to achieve academic success. They know how to make an A in all their other classes. They know how the system works and how to work the system. Suddenly they find themselves in a class that asks them to explore how they know what they know. Their concrete perception of the world gets a bit fuzzy. I have watched honor roll students struggle with this class because the boundaries were vague and I could not tell them with the precision of their chemistry teacher how to achieve an A. As a result, I have watched more than one such student unravel.

This is not to say that we should not care about grades at all, and Rocha concedes this. No one should try to earn a low mark. On the other hand, he suggests that "you should not confuse this institutionalized process of grade-getting, school-going, degree-worshipping, and job-seeking with what philosophy and education have to offer you."[91] While he admits that these things are not trivial or unimportant, his point is simply that there is something more to the enterprise than these things alone, and he uses a powerful analogy to make his point.

"It would be like trying to fall in love and get married in order to pay lower taxes,"[92] he writes. "[L]ower tax rates simply come as happy accidents. Likewise, good grades come as happy accidents, too."[93]

If making the honor roll or landing a job is not the supreme goal of education, what is? It is that little thing that caused Pontius Pilate to pause in wonder. Says Rocha, "Read for the truth. Write and speak to show what seems true. Ask questions to get at what might be true. Attend classes to seek the truth. Do not settle for shallow, impoverished grades and cheap, degrading rewards. Philosophy and education require courage."[94]

A Culture of Fear and Distrust

66

Not only is there something much greater in the purpose of education than merely attaining a grade or finding a job, but there is a genuine danger in focusing exclusively on those things. As Samuel Rocha points out in *A Primer for Philosophy & Education*, "The problem with grades, credentials, and formal schooling in general is that it often generates a culture and mentality of fear, distrust, and paranoia. Worst of all, it erodes what is truly worthwhile, replacing what is serious with a joke."[95]

I once had the opportunity of hearing Michael Wesch, a cultural anthropologist from Kansas State University, speak at a conference. After he delivered the keynote talk at lunch, I was eager to attend his breakout session in the afternoon, and it was there that he made a statement similar to that quoted above. He said, "We don't live in a culture of trust. That's why we're always assessing and assessing."

Yes, students do need to be assessed. It is right that a teacher sees what a student has learned and how well a student has learned it. Yes, teachers and administrators need to be evaluated. It is fair for an employer to know whether employees are fulfilling the tasks for which they have been hired.

Yet fear and distrust are at the heart of our obsessive worship at the altar of data. They both fuel it and are a consequence of it. We do not trust that people hired to do a job are actually doing it, so we must check up on them. We fear that someone will blame us because our students have not learned something, so we assess them. And then we do it again. And then we report the results to each other and talk about them. And then we assess again. And when it is all said and done, we report the final scores to others who can assess whether we have been doing the job for which we were hired, despite that our students have a free will and perform in ways that are influenced by factors beyond our control. Students walk around with the perfectly reasonable assumption that assessment and grades are the be-all, end-all of education, which leads them to a toxic level of stress. That toxicity spreads among the faculty who likewise have little choice but to believe that their role in society is actually capable of being measured by instruments better suited in the natural sciences.

But can a teacher or a student truly be evaluated in such ways? Rocha asks it like this. "Can one know all the information of a 'self' – physical details, family tree, likes and dislikes, and more – and claim to truly *know* that self?"[96] This is a central question in philosophy of mind and studies in artificial intelligence. The classic statement of it is in the form of a thought experiment by Frank Jackson,[97] which runs, in a grossly simplified way, as follows. Imagine Mary, who has spent her entire life in a black and white room. She learns everything there is to know about light and how the human eye and brain perceive and interpret light, and therefore color. There is no aspect of color that she does not know from a physical perspective, but she has never actually seen a color like red. One day, she is let out of her room and for the first time she sees red. The question then is whether or not she learns anything new or merely experiences what she already knows in a new way.

There are profound implications for artificial intelligence in this question, and philosophers of mind are lined up on both sides of the answer. It is a question that must be answered within education as well. If we think that Mary learns no new thing and that she merely experiences old knowledge in a new way, then we are committed to the belief that the physical description of a thing completely defines it. From this we can confidently assess students and teachers with tools and methods derived from the natural sciences. If, on the other hand, we believe that Mary does learn something genuinely novel, then we must admit that the complete picture of a thing cannot be had by listing only certain, quantifiable facts.

The fear and distrust that have produced our current obsession with assessment are reasonable, given the human condition. We fear and distrust many things. The fear and distrust that result from our hyper-evaluative culture, however, are the consequence, at least partially, from a conflicted reality. There is a deep, intuitive sense in us that Mary does learn something genuinely new, but when we are led to believe that this is not so and that the complete picture of a person can be had through quantitative assessment, the resultant dissonance becomes a significant contributor to the fear, distrust, and paranoia that grip our culture.

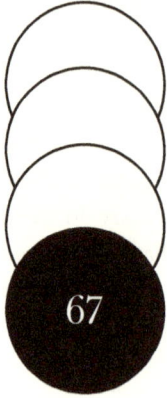

67   **Truth in Love**

In the fourth chapter of his letter to the Ephesians, St. Paul encouraged them to speak the truth in love. We usually, and rightly, see this as a statement on method. The admonishment to speak the truth in love reminds us that the truth can be spoken in ugliness and hatefulness, but that truth spoken in love is more likely to be received.

There is another sense in which this can be taken, one that recognizes the truth that exists and has its foundation in love, and it is this sense that is operative in the conclusion of Samuel Rocha's book *A Primer for Philosophy & Education*. After making the distinction between knowing and understanding, he continues by explaining the nature of the difference. "Understanding is beyond the scope of knowledge because it requires more than knowing, it requires being – *being in love*."[98]

I imagine that for some this will seem a bit of a letdown. Love is so common, so basic an idea, and we are always on the lookout for the new and exotic. Coming to the end of the book and finding this may be a little disappointing. It also does not seem very philosophical. There is the belief that philosophy is about heady things, and we think perhaps he would have done better to have ended the sentence above with "it requires being." That is suitably abstract. That has the proper ring of intellectual mystery.

Yet Rocha will have none of that. His philosophy is no incorporeal, wraithlike proposition. It is an incarnate thing, and he will not let us off the hook so easily. He continues, "When we drink from the font of wisdom we are filled with more than wisdom itself: we acquire understanding. By understanding, we become more than wise philosophers and sage educators. We become persons; we are personalized."[99]

There it is, the heart of this humane enterprise called education. As I have noted before, the etymology of "education" shows us that it is a work of leading out, presumably, following the illustration of Plato, a leading out of darkness and into light. "Lead," however, is a transitive verb, as is *ducere* in Latin, and it invites us to consider what is its proper direct object. In the case of education, this can be none other than people, human beings, us. We are the direct object. We lead each other on that grand journey of discovery, and what we discover is our humanity. As Rocha says, we become persons—we are personalized.

Whatever else may be said of us, this much is true. "Persons fundamentally desire and require love: to love and be loved. Without love, there is no understanding. Without love, there is nothing."[100]

This is an idea I have heard before. When she was inducted into the New Albany High School Hall of Fame, my Latin teacher, Alice Ranck Hettle, had this to say. "It is our responsibility as educators to provide a sound education based on ethical principles. Innate within every human being is first the desire to be noticed and to be loved, then comes the need to be taught to learn how to learn. It is the role of the teacher to notice and yes, to love the student so much that he is ready to learn, and in turn develop all of his potential. What better way for a teen-ager to learn to live honorably and well than to read from the literary masterpieces of Cicero."

Samuel Rocha and Miss Ranck (the name by which I will always know one of the true inspirations in my professional life) clearly mean more here than kind affection. This rich, robust love without which nothing exists cannot be described in a few paragraphs. Quite likely, it cannot be described with words at all. It can be glimpsed, and while we cannot embrace such a vast and deep entity, we can be embraced by it and in the true freedom of its limitless space we can come to know, to understand, and finally to be. For those wrestling with the educational challenges of our day, this should bring profound hope.

"This is where philosophy and life begin: in love. This is also where philosophy and education begin anew," says Rocha.[101] And to this I would add it is also in love where meaning is ultimately found in teaching.

Pieces of Advice

These Are Your Arts: Advice to Veteran Teachers

One of the most often told stories from the world of sports involves Vince Lombardi and the Green Bay Packers in 1961.[102] After watching the Packers lose the NFL championship game the previous season, Coach Lombardi launched the new season's practice with something unexpected by professional football players. He went back to the basics. Holding a football in front of the men, the coach announced, "This is a football," and from there led them through a review of game fundamentals they had known since they were children. At the end of that season, the Packers won the NFL championship against the New York Giants.

You are not just a professional teacher, but a veteran educator. You have a fair number of years of experience under your belt and have likely given presentations, led professional development sessions, and perhaps mentored several younger teachers. Unlike the 1961 Packers, you may have finished your most recent year of teaching with success. Even so, it is time to remember what a football is.

Why are you doing this? When did you hear the call to be a teacher?

Some hear that call early in life, and that is what leads them into the classroom. Others become teachers because they need the money or are biding their time until their dream job arrives, but then, somewhere along the way, they hear the call. If you have been teaching for a significant amount of time, you cannot still be doing so only for the paycheck and you surely are not still biding your time. Why, then, are you doing this?

Be brutally honest and tell yourself the reasons that do not keep you in the classroom. Think back, but not too long and hard, about the failures and challenges you have faced. Call to mind the major and minor injustices and indignities you have endured. Now ask yourself again, "Why am I still here?"

This will undoubtedly lead you to memories of certain wonderful students and delightful colleagues, but go a bit deeper. Students and colleagues come and go, so it is unlikely that particular people are the reason you have stayed with your calling. What is it about the grand object of education that keeps you coming back morning after morning, week after week, year after year?

Whatever that is, how will you hold onto it? As the Mother Superior said of Maria in *The Sound of Music*, how do you hold a moonbeam in your hand? The grand things of life, the true, the good, and the beautiful things, are as difficult to grasp as that moonbeam, and you know this. How many times have you felt the pressures of grading and meetings and people needing something from you every moment of the day threatened to steal your joy? The Roman philosopher Seneca famously observed that the reason people do not really feel better after a vacation is that they have not dealt with the reasons they needed one in the first place,[103] so, in addition to the minor, self-medicating strategies you have developed to get through the week, ask yourself and your fellow veteran colleagues what part of the grand object still inspires you.

Or, put it another way. When the Trojan hero Aeneas visits his father in the underworld in Book VI of Vergil's *Aeneid*, he receives a vision of what will one day be the Roman empire. His father points out to him that others will carve marble, be better orators, and map the motions of the stars, but that it will be the task of Romans to rule with authority and to establish peace. He concludes by saying, "*Hae tibi erunt artes.*"[104] "These will be your arts." What are yours?

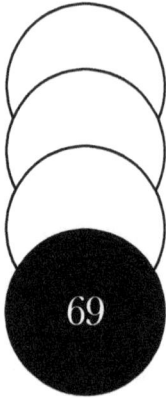

Preparing for Class: Advice to New Teachers

The best advice I can give those of you entering upon the great and noble calling of teaching comes from Montaigne's essay "Of Experience," which in Donald Frame's classic translation runs as follows.

I take great pleasure in seeing an army general, at the foot of a breach he means to attack presently, lending himself wholly and freely to his dinner and his conversation, among his friends, and Brutus, with heaven and earth conspiring against him and Roman liberty, stealing some hour of night from his rounds to read and annotate Polybius with complete assurance. It is for little souls, buried under the weight of business, to be unable to detach themselves cleanly from it or to leave it and pick it up again.[105]

With all that you are facing as you prepare to enter a classroom for the first time, or a class you have never taught, or a new school, it may seem as if you are going off to war. There are so many details to attend to regarding supplies and procedures and lessons. Yet Montaigne was correct. Only the small soul allows itself to be buried by such things, and yours can be no small soul if you have answered the call to teach.

How, then, will you maintain your focus on the greater things? It is unlikely that you will read and annotate the Greek historian Polybius, but what will you read? What music or art will you enjoy? Will you go for a walk? Will you enjoy the outdoors, whether on the night before your first day of school or your first weekend? Perhaps it will be dinner and conversation with friends, but if so, then do as Montaigne described and lend yourself wholly and freely to them, not rehearsing all you have yet to do behind the smile you show to others.

At the same time, remember that both in the classroom and in your outside, restorative activities, you are lending yourself and not giving yourself. The Roman Stoic philosopher Seneca offers a good word here. He writes, "*Ubicumque sum, ibi meus sum. Rebus enim me non trado, sed commodo.*"[106] "Wherever I am, I am my own. For I do not surrender myself to things, but loan myself."

Along with this, make friends with veteran teachers who can guide you and answer questions that you never even thought to ask before you entered a classroom. They will cheer your successes, stand by you in your failures, and point the way as you grow as a teacher. It is crucial, however, to associate more closely with those who find joy in what they do than with those who are looking for someone to share their own misery or, even worse, someone they can persuade to their side in some Byzantine plot of building politics. Avoid the latter at all costs.

Speak often with your administrators. Ask them questions, not just about school-related issues, but about their lives. You will appreciate it when they show an interest in you in addition to what you bring to the school, and they will be glad as well when you do the same.

Become part of your school's life beyond what you do in the classroom. Buy some apparel that advertises your school right away and look for opportunities to wear it. Attend student activities. Start a club or quickly say yes if a student asks you to sponsor one. Even if you do not know everything about the activity, remember that you are smart and capable. You will figure it out as you go.

And when, not if, you become overwhelmed, remember that you have loaned yourself to any given activity, not surrendered yourself to it. You can leave something undone. You can always do it tomorrow.

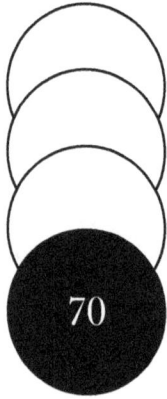

Equal Danger: Advice to Administrators

I have to admit that I was wrong about you. Early in my career I was looking at two different schools in which to teach, and someone had told me that the administration was better at one of them. I remember thinking that this did not matter, for once I was in my classroom, I would be in my own little world. All that mattered were the students. That, however, was profoundly naïve, for through direct experience with administrators in schools where I have taught to observations of others, along with a deepening understanding of leadership throughout history, I have come to see that what you do matters very much in creating and maintaining the atmosphere of a school.

It was the fall of 325 B.C. when Alexander the Great led his massive army back toward Greece across the Gedrosian Desert. Water was scarce, but when some was found, a soldier brought a helmet filled with it to Alexander. The great king in turn poured out its contents onto the sand, unwilling to drink when his soldiers could not.

In 58 B.C., Julius Caesar led the Roman legions in a battle with the Gallic people called the Helvetians. At the Battle of Bibracte, Caesar writes that he wanted all the horses sent away so that the danger would be equal for all and no one would have the means to flee the fight. He adds that he dismissed his own horse first.[107]

Just a few years later after the Roman civil war between Caesar and Pompey, a famous and respected senator named Cato led Roman troops home across the desert sands of North Africa. The poet Lucan memorialized Cato's leadership in these lines.

> Thus let me be the first to step upon the burning sand,
> The first whom blazing sun may strike in this snake-
> poisoned land,
> And from my fate you well may see what dangers are
> at hand.
> Then let him thirst who sees me drink, who sees me
> seek the shade.
> Let him alone faint with the heat or fall, if on parade
> He sees me ride before the troops while they as yet
> march on,
> For whether I command or serve, I would not have it
> known.[108]

The best building- and district-level leaders I have known have been from the mold of Alexander, Caesar, and Cato. They have shared the challenges of educating children along with the teachers. They have inspired them, worked beside them, and always supported them with an encouraging word or deed.

How obvious would it be to an outsider whether you lead or serve? Are you regularly in the hallways and classrooms of your buildings, not just to observe but to build relationships with students and teachers and to support all in what they do?

How do you conduct meetings? Do you insist on the trappings of position by standing on a stage and looking down at your teachers? One principal under whom I taught scheduled coffees every other month, and rather than requiring the whole faculty to meet at once, invited us in small groups during our prep periods to meet and share a drink. It meant the usual, one-hour faculty meeting took his whole day, but he was willing to do that to provide a different, more meaningful experience for the teachers.

Why are you in the position you hold? Was it merely for the increase in pay, or do you, as hopefully your teachers do, hold to a grand vision of education and understand your role of fostering an environment in which it can be achieved?

It is often said that leadership is lonely. Who in your school can speak truth to you? To whom can you speak truthfully? When the ancient Romans called on one of their own to take command of the army in a crisis, they appointed that person a second in command to advise and support him. Even Batman had Robin. Who is that for you?

Unfortunately, the clearest evaluation of your leadership will take place after your teachers and students have left your building, and it is simply this. Do they choose to come back to visit? Do they maintain contact with you? One of the surest signs of corporate dysfunction is when all the employees park with their cars facing outward from the spaces in order to get away as quickly as possible at the end of the day.

71 Back-to-School Life: Advice to Parents

You may have enjoyed school and you may not have, but unless you are an educator, you probably did not think you would be going back to it, at least not in any meaningful way beyond the occasional reunion. Yet here you are, a parent to a young person for whom education and most likely formal schooling will occupy the lion's share of waking hours. If you thought this would involve little more from you than the annual back-to-school night, you will need to think again. Welcome to back-to-school life.

There will always be supplies you need to purchase and various forms to complete, but if you want your child to get the most out of his or her education, then your responsibility will go beyond those basics. This will undoubtedly involve doing things that you may not like, may not be interested in, or may be too tired to do. Then again, you probably do not like driving your children to all of their various sport and music practices. You may well not be interested in watching every single minute of one of their events, and it is more than likely that you have attended some of those events in the walking exhaustion known only to parents. And yet you have done so, and so you must when it comes to their education. As a teacher who has worked with parents for decades, I have seen much that is successful and much that is not. What follows are my suggestions.

Read

We do not need more studies to tell us what common sense suggests, that excessive screen time is not good for the mental development of children. Many of us come home from work and simply want to go numb in front of the television, and no one is saying that you should never relax with a favorite show or movie. Yet you need to read, both to your children and for yourself in their presence. If your children are young, read to them at night before bed. In their earliest years this could be from a picture book that will capture their attention and show them that exciting things lie between the covers of books. As they grow older, a chapter or even part of a chapter from a young adult book would be appropriate. Recall books you enjoyed in your childhood. It is a special moment for both of you when you share favorite stories from when you were the same age as your child. And when your children observe you reading for pleasure from a print newspaper or book, not from a screen, they pick up the subtle message that this is a good thing and it is what adults do.

Understand Your Role

These are your children, and while it may be good for the rest of us that your children know certain things, at the end of the day, you are responsible for what they know, what they should be able to do, and how they should acquire such knowledge and skills. You may think you have fulfilled your requirements by sending your children to the local school, but you have choices, and it is up to you to make the best ones. Consider all the options, such as taxpayer-funded (public) schools, private schools, co-ops, hybrid schools, and homeschooling. No model is right for all people, and you must take into account the needs of your children along with your own abilities and resources. If you choose any model other than homeschooling, you need to find out about the adults who will be shaping the intellectual, moral, emotional, physical, and spiritual life of your children. Explore school websites and visit schools in person. Ask questions about what is taught and how, and if it all seems too daunting, ask a friend or relative in education to help you. The chances are good you know someone who is or has been a teacher, and that person will almost certainly be happy to help you navigate the questions and options.

Ask Your Children Questions

This does not need to be an interrogation, but you should know what goes on in your child's school day. It is not necessary that you recall all of the names of your child's teachers, although you are likely to do this with the names of your favorite professional athletes and entertainers, but you should know which teachers your child really likes and which he or she does not. Ask your children about specific classes, and if they are not able to tell you what is going on or when the next exam will take place, tell them to find out and tell you the next day. It is always appropriate to ask teachers questions, but if it is something that your child should reasonably know, help your child be the one to provide that information.

Help Your Children Prepare Daily

Most classes in middle school and high school will have regular assignments outside the school day, and this can extend to elementary school as well. Your children should be able to tell you what they need to do each day and whether they need your help doing it. This is where digging into your own inner reserve comes into play. You may need to grab your own after school snack to have the energy to focus on helping with assignments. You may need to stifle your own frustration with having to do one more thing at the end of your work day, for if you express your distaste for the work of learning, your children will develop a similar distaste. Your involvement in the educational life of your children will bring that education to life. If you know that from your own experience, you will want your children to have the same. If that was not what you experienced in your own education, would you not like for your own children to have something better?

Acknowledgements

It is rare that what pays the bills is also one's *raison d'etre*, but I am grateful to God that such has been the case for me with teaching. I want to thank all the amazing teachers I have known, both those in whose classes I sat as a student and those with whom I worked as a colleague. Were it not for my parents, teachers both, I would not have entered upon this delightful journey. Were it not for my wife, the best teacher I know, I would not be eagerly pursuing the many inviting turns on the path ahead. Great gratitude goes out to my friend Gary Abud, Jr., whose shepherding of this project has been all an author could ever desire. I also want to thank especially my son, Austin, with whom it has been the pleasure of a lifetime to collaborate on the layout of this book and whose work on its design is delightful and makes me more than just a little proud.

Notes

1   Korzybski, Alfred. *Manhood Of Humanity: The Science and Art of Human Engineering*. E.P. Dutton & Co., 1918.

2   in.gov/history/2883.htm

3   Lines 97-98

4   Montaigne. *The Complete Essays of Montaigne*. Translated by Donald Frame, Stanford University Press, 1965. pp. 89-90.

5   Plato. *Republic*. Translated by Benjamin Jowett, Modern Library, 1982. pp. 182-184.

6   Seneca. *Seneca: Six Tragedies*. Translated by Emily Wilson, Oxford University Press, 2010. p. vii.

7   zhaolearning.com/2014/09/13/fatal-attraction-americas-suicidal-quest-for-educational-excellence/

8   Mommsen, Theodor. *The History of Rome*. Translated by Dero A. Saunders and John H. Collins, Meridian Books, 1956. p. 1.

9 All statistics from statista.com

10 *Ab Urbe Condita*, I.25

11 ncregister.com/blog/anthony-esolen-in-his-own-words-why-i-left-providence-college-for-thomas-more

12 crisismagazine.com/opinion/left-providence-college

13 crisismagazine.com/opinion/left-providence-college

14 Lockwood, Dean. "Two Thousand Years of Latin Translation from the Greek." *Transactions of the American Philological Association*, vol. 49, 1918, pp. 115-129.

15 The two digitized copies can be found at: archive.org/details/bub_gb_ucju1UXVU9UC/page/n3/mode/2up and babel.hathitrust.org/cgi/pt?id=ucm.5327265235&view=1up&seq=5.

16 Hamilton, Edith. *Mythology*. Warner Books, 1965. pp. 89-90.

17 https://poets.org/poem/because-you-asked-about-line-between-prose-and-poetry

18 Lines 9-10

19 *Pro Archia*, 14

20 This idea of embodying what one teaches is discussed beautifully and in considerable detail in *Lessons of the Masters* by George Steiner.

21 wsj.com/articles/teachers-are-quitting-

and-companies-are-hot-to-hire-them-11643634181

22   time.com/5769431/mummy-speaks-voice/

23   Sokal, Alan. "Transgressing the Boundaries: Towards a Transformative Hermeneutics of Quantum Gravity." *Social Text*, vol. #46/47, 1989, pp. 217-252.

24   The creators of this website discuss the background for their work in Bullhak, Andrew. "On the Simulation of Postmodernism and Mental Debility Using Recursive Transition Networks." *Monash University Department of Computer Science Technical Report*, 1996.

25   documentacatholicaomnia.eu/

26   In 2022, NASA converted pressure waves emanating from a black hole into sounds that humans could hear. youtube.com/watch?v=FMifNQ7MFMU

27   "Epitaph for Sir Isaac Newton," lines 1-2

28   *Flatland* is an 1884 novella that, while offering commentary on Victorian culture, explores what life would be like in worlds with only one, two, three, and four dimensions.

29   Thorne, Kip. "Wormholes in Spacetime and Their Use for Interstellar Travel: A Tool for Teaching General Relativity." *American Journal of Physics*, vol. 56, 1988, pp. 395-416.

30   thepublicdiscourse.com/2017/02/18617/

31   According to the *Guinness Book of World Records*, this happened in 1972 when the hard rock band Deep Purple played the Rainbow Theatre in London. https://books.google.com/

32   forbes.com/sites/lizryan/2016/03/07/ten-unmistakable-signs-of-a-bad-place-to-work/?sh=f09a01676356

33   Thucydides. *Thucydides.* Translated by Benjamin Jowett, vol. 1, Oxford University Press, 1881. p. xx.

34   "To Virgil," lines 37-40

35   Aristotle. *The Poetics of Aristotle.* Translated by Samuel Butcher, 2nd ed., Macmillan and Co., 1896. p. 49.

36   *Preuves par discours I*, Laf. 423, Sel. 680 penseesdepascal.fr/II/II1-moderne.php

37   See T.S. Eliot's "The Love Song of J. Alfred Prufrock," line 114.

38   In Book II.216-224 of his *De Rerum Natura* (*On the Nature of Things*), the Roman poet and Epicurean philosopher Lucretius (c. 99-c. 55 B.C.) wrote of atoms descending in straight lines with the occasional and unexplainable swerve that allowed them to connect with other atoms and produce matter.

39   Steiner, George. *Lessons of the Masters.* 2nd ed., Harvard University Press, 2005. p. 16.

40   Ibid., p. 17.

41   Ibid., p. 19.

42   Ibid., p. 70.

43   Psalm 119:14

44   Steiner, p. 72.

45   Ibid., p. 75.

46   "Andrea del Sarto," lines 97-98

47   founders.archives.gov/documents/Franklin/01-01-02-0011

48   Nyssa, Gregory. *"De Deitate Filii Et Spiritus Sancti."* *Patrologiae Graecae*, vol. Tomus xlvi, 1855, p. 558b.

49   in.gov/history/about-indiana-history-and-trivia/explore-indiana-history-by-topic/indiana-documents-leading-to-statehood/constitution-of-1816/article-ix/

50   s3.us-east-2.amazonaws.com/iga-publications/indiana_constitution/Archive%20Constitution%20(as%20amended%202018).pdf

51   *"Ceteros pudeat, si qui se ita litteris abdiderunt ut nihil possint ex eis neque ad communem adferre fructum, neque in aspectum lucemque proferre."* *Pro Archia*, 12

52   *Academica* II.XLI.127

53   nytimes.com/2017/11/02/magazine/the-first-woman-to-translate-the-odyssey-into-english.html

54   *Pro Archia*, 12

55   shepherdcommunity.org

56   wildmanandsteve.com

57   youtube.com/watch?v=S_6ftpXSLiY

58   *Hamlet*, Act 1, Scene 4

59   Bertie Wooster is the fictional character created by P.G. Wodehouse who features in a series of novels and in the mid-1990s television series *Jeeves & Wooster*.

60   *Pharsalia* IX.392-394

61   "...siquo fuerit discrimine notum dux an miles eam...." *Pharsalia* IX.401-402

62   Mack, Maynard. *Alexander Pope: A Life*. W.W. Norton & Co., 1988. pp. 44-47.

63   Johnson, Samuel. *Life of Pope*. Edited by Peter Peterson, Macmillan and Co., 1899. p. 23.

64   Pope, Alexander. *The Iliad of Homer*. Edited by Steven Shankman, Penguin Books, 1994. p. 26.

65   Ibid., p. 231.

66   midtownscholar.com/

67   abc.net.au/news/2014-07-29/canberra-65-returns-from-week-at-us-space-camp/5633036

68   cla.purdue.edu/alumni/awards/distinguished-alumni-archive/2015/kathy-nimmer.html

69   Galilei, Galileo. *Il Saggiatore*. 1623. p. 25. This is a popular paraphrase. Galileo's actual words were, "*Egli u scritto in lingua matematica, e i caratteri son triangoli, cerchi, & altre figure Geometriche, senza i quali mezi u imponibile a intenderne umanamente parola.*" "It [i.e., the universe] was written in the language of mathematics, and its letters are triangles, circles, and other geometric figures, without which it is impossible by human means

to understand a word." archive.org/details/bub_gb_pB29UzJf1DwC/page/n39/mode/2up

70   "To His Coy Mistress," line 1

71   Established in 1936 and serving middle school and high school students in Classics courses, the National Junior Classical League is one of the oldest student youth organizations in the world. To read more about it, visit njcl.org.

72   The American Classical League is a professional organization for teachers of Classics. To read more about it, visit aclclassics.org.

73   The Classical Association of the Middle West and South is a professional organization for teachers of Classics. To read more about it, visit camws.org.

74   craigallenjohnson.com

75   centerofthewest.org

76   Perkins, Steven R. "From Servius to Advanced Placement: The Anfractuous Path of the Helen Episode in *Aeneid* 2." *The Classical Outlook*, vol. 89, no. 4, 2012, p. 113.

77   John 14:6

78   Rocha, Samuel. *A Primer for Philosophy & Education*. CreateSpace, 2013. All references to *A Primer for Philosophy & Education* are from this edition. A later edition was published by Wipf and Stock in 2014.

79   Rocha, page ii.

80   Ibid., ii-iii

81   Plantinga, Alvin. "Advice to Christian Philosophers." *Faith and Philosophy: Journal of the Society of Christian Philosophers*, vol. 1, no. 3, 1984, pp. 253-271.

81   Rocha, p. 3

82   Ibid., p. 4

83   rogerebert.com/reviews/spirit-stallion-of-the-cimarron-2002

84   Rocha, p. 10.

85   Ibid, pp. 14, 15.

86   Ibid., pp. 16.

87   Ibid., p. 20.

88   Rocha, p. 20.

89   Ibid.

90   Ibid., pp. 30, 31.

91   Ibid., p. 31.

92   Ibid., p. 33.

93   Ibid., pp. 33-34.

94   Ibid., p. 34.

95   Ibid., 33.

96   Rocha, p. 37

97   Jackson, Frank. "What Mary Didn't Know." *The Journal of Philosophy*, vol. 83, no. 5, 1987, pp. 291-295.

98   Rocha., p. 42.

99   Ibid., p. 43.

100   Ibid., p. 43.

101   Ibid., p. 44.

102   edmondbusiness.com/2021/02/gentlemen-this-is-a-football

103   *Epistulae ad Lucilium* **XXVIII**

104   *Aeneid* **VI**.852

105   Montaigne. *The Complete Essays of Montaigne*. Translated by Donald Frame, Stanford University Press, 1965. p. 851.

106   *Epistulae ad Lucilium* **LXII**

107   *De Bello Gallico*, I.25

108   *Pharsalia* IX.395-402

Index

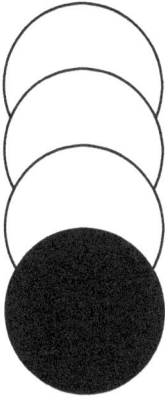

About the Author

Steve is a native Hoosier from New Albany, Indiana. He earned a B.A. with honors in Classical Studies at Indiana University and an M.A. in Classics from The University of Texas. He has taught Latin for nearly thirty-five years in a variety of settings, including an urban middle school in Kansas City, Missouri, and at undergraduate and high school levels in Texas. In Indiana, he has taught Latin and Classics courses at North Central High School and Butler University, and since 2021 he has taught Latin at Guerin Catholic High School in Noblesville, Indiana. He is the author of numerous books and articles in the field of Classical Studies, including the popular *Latin For Dummies*. In addition to being the 2014 Indiana Teacher of the Year, Steve is a recipient of The College of Wooster Excellence in Teaching Award, the Lilly Teacher Creativity Fellowship, the Dr. Elizabeth Watkins Latin Teacher Award from the American Classical League, and is a Texas Foreign Language Association Latin Teacher of the Year. He is also a member of Phi Kappa Phi and Phi Beta Kappa and in 2014 was named a Sagamore of the Wabash by Governor Mike Pence. When he is not teaching and writing, he loves spending time with his wife Melissa and their children Austin and Olivia.

www.ingramcontent.com/pod-product-compliance
Lightning Source LLC
Chambersburg PA
CBHW021138090426
42740CB00008B/840